artdigilandbooks **interviews**

HIRO NARITA. DEPTH OF FIELD
Life and Work of a Cinematographer

curated by Gerry Guida
preface by Carroll Ballard

art digiland

art digiland

Artdigiland Ltd
Registered office: c/o Raheny Accounts Ltd TA
6 Abbey Business Park, Baldoyle Industrial Estate,
Dublin 13, Rep. of Ireland
Sede operativa Italia: via Clelia 53, 00181 Roma
www.artdigiland.com
info@artdigiland.com

Hiro Narita. Depth of Field
Life and Work of a Cinematographer
curated by Gerry Guida

editor: Ken Hurry
book design: Francesca Giannotta

photographic credits: Hiro Narita (pages 26, 29, 66, 74, 190, 192), Barbara Parker Narita (pages 36, 38, 39, 42, 44, 65, 67, 71), Pictures & Words (page 34), Pamela Gentile (pages 93, 169), American Cinematographer (pages 104, 108, 110), Charlie Kuttner (page 141), Disney Pictures (page 96), American Zoetrope (pages 165, 167), Karman Muller (pages 165, 167), ILM (page 219)

opposite page, Hiro Narita, photo by Rebekah Koa

cover: Hiro Narita on the set of *Late Lunch* by Eleanor Coppola. Photo by Karman Muller (courtesy of American Zoetrope)

©2023 Artdigiland

Summary

11	**Preface by Carroll Ballard**
13	**Origins and Studies**
24	**Documentary to narrative** 1970s-1980s
62	**Indies to Studios** 1980s-1990s
101	**Hollywood** 1990s-2000s
153	**San Francisco** 2000s-2010s
164	**Without border** 2010s-2020s
171	**Considerations on the cinema and beyond**
	Testimonials
198	Lucille Carra
199	Eleanor Coppola
199	Lynn Hershman Leeson
200	Scott Farrar, ASC
200	Bruce Nicholson
202	**Filmography**
220	**Awards & Nominations**

Preface

The original story of *Never Cry Wolf* takes place in the Arctic Wasteland of Northern Canada.

After reconnoitering, a specific location was found in the vast Yukon Territories, where, over a hundred years ago, the Klondike Sourdoughs grubbed for gold. There, I proposed we shoot the film using a crew of folks that had never been North of the 60th parallel, whose ideas of snow and ice, storms and isolation were based on ski trips in California.

So I wondered, who can I choose to shoot this film? The cinematographer will be the key man. He must be even-tempered, considerate and cool. He must be adaptable to radical changes in conditions, he must be flexible and inventive, able to improvise when things get difficult and chaotic. He should have clear ideas of the objectives we are seeking to realize and, on top of it all, he must have a good 'eye' to find the special, the beautiful, and the most moving images to present before the lens.

After considering some of the most talented shooters I knew, I was still in a quandary.

Then, by chance I saw some of Hiro Narita's earlier work and, after hanging out with him for a short time it became clear to me that - this was the guy!

As it turned out, this was one of the most fortunate decisions I ever made!

Carroll Ballard

Origins and Studies

You were born in Seoul, South Korea on June 26 1941. When World War II ended your family was evacuated to Nara, Japan, where you lived for a few years before moving to Tokyo. Your father Masuo Morikawa was a doctor who hoped you would become one too. Unfortunately, he died when you were just 12. Your mother Masako then remarried a Japanese American. What do you remember from your childhood?

As soon as the war ended my family evacuated from Seoul, Korea, to Japan with the bare necessities we could carry. Like flashes of images from a flip book, my memory of the period is both vivid and blurred. In spite of the meager living conditions, we re-established our life in Nara, once the ancient capital of Japan and the roots of the Morikawa family from generations back. The city, thankfully, had been spared from the air raids, and my father managed to set up a modest clinic, a far cry from the hospital he managed in Seoul. But his big dream to launch a hospital in Tokyo took us on a move again. Along with visible signs of recovery in the country, my father's medical practice saw its own upswing, only to be cut short by his early death from illness. Before he passed away. I know my father assumed, if not wished, I would follow his vocation as he did his father's. But I felt indifferent to his medical profession: it was remote from my heart; instead, drawing pictures or building toys preoccupied my childhood, and my future remained vague. My mother, at age 37 with four children in tow, held minuscule jobs and persevered, but at one point, she decided to convert my father's clinic into rental units and studio apartments in hope of a better life. Eventually though, she accepted an arranged marriage to Dr. Narita in Honolulu, Hawaii. Over the span of 12 years encompassing three countries, so many events unfolded before my eyes that I learned to come to terms with the fact that wherever I am is where I belong: my home. In retrospect, the borders between countries and cultures became less defined in my mind, more intertwined in the years to come.

Hiro Narita: young boy before evacuation (1944)

origins and studies

Your real family name is Morikawa?

My biological family name Morikawa, I believe, stems from western Japan, but I was told my father was born in Tokyo, indicating the Morikawas in the last few generations moved far and wide. Some relatives settled as far away as Manchuria. The name denotes forest (mori) and river (kawa); a description of the dominant landscape around the dwellers, adopted as their surname; a common practice in Japan through the centuries. My ancestors, I assume, were farmers or loggers.

Where does Narita originate?

Narita is also a conventional surname, as in the name of the city Narita where Narita International Airport is located near Tokyo. Nari or Naru is to grow and Ta is field: growing field, like rice field.

Do you have any brothers or sisters?

Of four siblings my oldest sister and I were adopted by Dr. Narita, but my 2nd older sister was adopted by another family in central Japan with my younger brother accompanying her as a foster child for the time being. He retained the family name Morikawa, and when he reached 18, joined us in Hawaii. By then my stepfather had died and I had already moved to San Francisco for school. Like a river, my life was in constant flux.

Did you all meet up again?

My wife and I saw my sister in Japan just once while visiting there. It was the only time I saw her since I left Japan thirty years earlier. As polite as we were to each other at the reunion–she had changed or I had changed so much–I felt we were almost strangers. My wife understood that my sister and I had gone through very unlikely paths and that our childhood memories were buried too deeply to recover. Even so, I feel close to her children, who studied in the US, and we have been keeping contact. My sister passed away a decade ago, but I see my other siblings time to time. They both left Hawaii and live on the mainland now.

In 1957, while you were in high school, you moved to Hawaii (Honolulu), when you graduated from Kaimuki High School. You then won a four-year scholarship to study at a school of your choice, choosing the San Francisco Art Institute, where you received a BFA in Graphic Design in 1964. What can you tell me about your school years?

My art teacher in high school, Mr. Richard Kim, was very supportive of my artistic inclination and, recognizing my limited English skills and how much adjustment I needed in my new country, suggested I explore and plow my path in a visual arts school when I graduate, rather than going to university. At the time, I was toying with the idea of becoming a painter or an architect, the notion only vaguely formed in my mind until I received a scholarship from San Francisco Art Institute. And I enrolled in the Graphic Design department; this was speculative, yet I felt it was a realistic choice, a better chance to earn a living in the future owing to its tangible applications in society. An additional benefit to me, the Graphic Design curriculum included several fine arts courses. Figurative painters like Richard Diebenkorn and Elmer Bischoff, and photographer Imogen Cunningham were on the faculty, inspiring a generation of art students. It was an favorable time and I immersed myself in that exciting, fertile ground, absorbing everything I could muster, and the four years of study rolled past quickly. By then I was almost certain that I would become a graphic designer. Decades later I discovered that many art students at the SF Institute emerged as film directors, editors, sound designers, and cinematographers; in retrospect, a reasonable, logical evolution of the visual artists, I thought.

origins and studies

During your years of study at the San Francisco Art Institute, as you said you had classmates who later worked in the film industry. Can you tell me any names?

I can name several who studied at the Institute over the years. Director Katherine Bigelow (*The Hurt Locker*), sound designer Richard Beggs (*Children of Men, Lost in Translation*)–he was my class-

Hiro Narita's family in Nara, around 1947

mate and I remember taking slides of his paintings for his portfolio–visual effects supervisor Gary Gutierrez (*The Right Stuff*), cinematographer Lance Acord (*Lost in Translation*), and so on.

When you were a child, what film made the strongest impression on you?

War-torn Japan gave us little options for amusement or entertainment; maybe baseball and movies. Movies were abundant and a child could enter a movie house with a few coins. In Tokyo I went to see them alone or with my father with very little understanding of what they were all about. Many American and European films filled theaters as well, and I remember seeing Jean Gabin, Maria Schell, and Errol Flynn in awe–I learned their names much later–but the titles and the stories escape me now. I was often glued to the radio also. One evening, I heard an interview with actress Kyo Machiko (*Ugetsu*). She was sharing her grueling experience during the filming of *Rashomon* directed by Akira Kurosawa, recounting how many times she had to repeat her screaming in a scene–I remember her scream over and over–till the director was satisfied. Somehow that broadcast stuck in the back of my head, as clear as yesterday's news, from a child's perspective, with baffled fascination.
These selective memories were stored away in my memory bank for years to come, and I can conjecture that such lasting imprints might have resurfaced and steered me to filmmaking.

After you graduated a few months later you got a job with documentary filmmaker John Korty, for illustrations and related tasks, but the Vietnam War intervened and so you were drafted and spent many months in the Pentagon's data information center making charts and graphs: overall you spent two years in the Army (1964-1966). What sparked your interest in Cinematography?

Just as I was finishing my studies at San Francisco Art Institute and working part time in a design studio, a young filmmaker -

origins and studies

John Korty - whom I first met at the Art Institute, stopped by and told us he was preparing his first feature film, *Crazy Quilt*. He was looking for a trainee, all-round production assistant who could also take stills, and even design promotional materials. Thrilled at the opportunity to learn filmmaking while contributing my skills, I decided to work for Korty with my employer's reassuring support. Regrettably, a few weeks into preproduction, I received my draft notice from the US Army and abruptly my dream job evaporated. Two years of interruption in my career followed, and I had to come to terms with this unfortunate situation quite beyond my control. Seeing many other draftees who had to leave their civilian lives under more complicated and adverse circumstances

Hiro Narita: the Basic Training, The US Army 1964

The training graduation 1964

than mine, I accepted the unsettling reality as a twist of fate.

To ease the emotional strain during my service I regularly went to movie theaters on weekends and increasingly began to gravitate toward cinema, not only for temporary distraction and entertainment, but for inspiration. Unlike graphic design I began to see that a sequence of moving images had so much potential in exploring human emotions and telling complex stories. Around that time a wave of works (some revivals) by great European directors were being screened in art-house marquees. Among these, I saw Antonioni's *Red Desert* and Bunuel's *The Exterminating Angel* which captivated me and boosted my interest.

This period was strangely reminiscent of my childhood in Japan. Movies were filling my emotional void; and actually, they were nurturing my life. As an Army specialist I was stationed in the Pentagon (the United States Military Headquarters), and my duty was to design charts and graphs–secret information included– for briefings held by high Army echelons. From the materials I worked on, I learned about a possible escalation of the war in Vietnam. Rumors were spreading quickly by then that our duty could be extended for another year. Anxiously, along with other soldiers, I performed my daily duty and counted the number of days left before my discharge, and going back to San Francisco to pursue my career.

On the brighter side, I came to know interesting people in the Army. In particular, I met a civilian computer programmer in my Data Information Command–while a roomful of giant computers would now fit into my lap-top or even iPhone–who suggested I should read Herman Hesse and recommended some movies I should watch. He even invited me to his family barbeque and chatted about art and life. I did not expect to meet people in the military who would help broaden my intellect and my mind. I realize now that teachers were everywhere, sometimes sitting behind an office desk or in uniform in a military building.

After my discharge from the Army–two years without extension– I asked John Korty to take me on as an apprentice. He agreed. Even so, there was a long road ahead of me and it took about

hiro narita. depth of field

ten more years of meandering to make the definite transition from graphic design to cinematography. Thinking back, it was my military service that cemented the direction of my career in filmmaking.

What was the movie that inspired you to become a cinematographer?

I saw *Knife in the Water* by Roman Polanski as a student and liked it very much, without any analytic or critical viewpoint. On seeing it again years later, I wondered what it was that struck me initially to think beyond the story. The images in the film made me aware of where the camera was positioned, giving me the best perspective, or the best seat in the house, so to speak. But, at times, some images were hidden from my view forcing my imagination to take over, to fill in. This precise, if not calculated,

Hiro Narita's painting from 1963 or 1964

visual articulation was a captivating element in *Knife in the Water*, and I realized then that cinematography is not just image-capturing, it is a vehicle to stir up psychological modulation in the viewer's mind.

Knife in the Water *(1961) marks Roman Polański's outstanding debut and was nominated for Best Foreign Language Film at the 1963 Academy Awards, the first Polish motion picture to receive this kind of recognition. The cinematography is by Jerzy Lipman, considered to be co-creator of the famous Polish Film School movement. His filming was very complex; in fact he had to capture many of the scenes with a hand-held Arri camera; continuity was also a big problem, as objects fluctuated constantly, given the marine setting, and slow-moving cloud formations were the main backdrop of the action obviously tumbling over the photography. What can you tell me about Lipman's work?*

I had to watch it again to gather my thoughts on Lipman's cinematography. The changing weather, the sun's shifting positions, and some variance in light were initially swept away by the strong current of the psychological drama. In fact, those visual mismatches, to which I did not pay attention particularly in the past, seemed to bring out emotional resonance and discord of the characters at certain moments. For instance, the rain–I loved it–added aggravating tensions to the unexpected turn of the plot. I am curious whether that segment of the film was scripted as rain or they had to accept the condition and alter the script, making the best of the situation. It is interesting that my reaction to the film changes over time, adding another layer to the old ones. I appreciated the many beautiful compositions, deceptively simple, which captured the physical and psychological tensions between the three characters in the small cramped boat. Much of the initial allure of the film to me over fifty years ago still remains vivid and sustained.

Documentary to narrative

1970s-1980s

Then you began freelancing as an assistant cameraman. You worked on a succession of low-budget films, but you also worked on a legendary film: Michelangelo Antonioni's Zabriskie Point *(1970).* Zabriskie Point *was the second of three feature films shot by Antonioni in English, and with foreign leading actors, produced by Carlo Ponti. The other two were* Blow-Up *(1966) and* The Passenger *(1975). For this film, the role of the two protagonists was entrusted by Antonioni to two non-professional rookies: Mark Frechette and Daria Halprin. Some of the film's scenes were shot on location at Zabriskie Point in Death Valley. The cinematography is by Alfio Contini AIC.*
How were you contacted?

Stepping-stones were all around me, often randomly placed. Out of necessity or choice, I jumped from one to the next simply to move forward and get experience. One day, Korty's inhouse producer asked me to film a quick screen test of a local stage actor for Michelangelo Antonioni, who was searching around the country for the key male role in his upcoming American film, *Zabriskie Point*. Korty was initially approached, but he was out of town and I was to fill in for him. Together with the producer, I filmed a short test on streets in San Francisco showing the actor's physical features, his body movements, some facial expressions, all without sound. Thinking it was just one-time job, I had no second thoughts.

documentary to narrative

What do you remember of your first meeting with Antonioni?

Antonioni was one of my favorite directors and I liked his earlier documentaries as well; his extraordinary sense of space, graphic composition, and stirring images always captivated me. Not long after the screen test, I received a call from producer Harrison Starr asking me to meet with Antonioni at his MGM office. Startled at first, I took courage and flew to Los Angeles. Antonioni explained that he needed to see on film the civil riots and student demonstrations that were gathering force in several major cities. I was honored to take on the assignment but I was self-conscious, even petrified, about meeting his expectations. He wanted these escalating outbreaks on film as reference, milieu, for *Zabriskie Point*, in which the storyline reflected the polarizing atmosphere of the time.

What do you remember of the moments you shot for your scenes?

The two major events, especially San Francisco State College's Third World Liberation Front demonstration and the anti-war demonstration surrounding the Chicago Democratic Convention, became the focus of my effort. Often, I was thrown into chaotic situations with waves of untethered demonstrators out of control. During these filming events, it might have occurred to me to echo Antonioni's perspective, but it was futile and a pretentious attempt on my part. I tried to remain an impartial documentary cinematographer, yet my subjective mind intruded sometimes. I have to admit that fact and fiction might have crisscrossed in my venture. I hoped at least that the images I took provided a texture, a mosaic of American culture during those turbulent moments. Producer Starr foresaw a state of uncontrolled frenzy and violence in Chicago and hired a young karate player as my bodyguard to push away demonstrators and stop them slamming into me and knocking my camera out of my hands. Aside from my protection, I trained him to be my assistant cameraman, reloading the film magazines when necessary. He was extraordi-

hiro narita. depth of field

narily efficient, and he made this unique experience even more memorable.

Is there any anecdote you can tell me?

I want to add a coincidence here. While I was filming the demonstrations in Chicago, I saw Haskell Wexler–I only knew of him through magazine articles and photographs–also filming in the midst of chaos. I learned later that he was directing *Medium Cool*, starring Peter Bonerz, the star of Korty's *Funnyman* for which I designed the movie poster. We first glanced at each other's cameras and saw they were not newsreel cameras (mine was an Arriflex C with a Panavision anamorphic short zoom lens and Wexler's was an Aaton CM3). We then exchanged discreet nods of recognition that we were not working for TV news, and we moved on our separate ways, blending with the demonstrators. Through the years since then Wexller and I have met on many occasions; at a seminar my wife organized for him for Women in Film festival and, as members, at the Cinematogra-

Director Michelangelo Antonioni on the movie set *Zabriskie Point* (1969).
Photo by Hiro Narita

documentary to narrative

phers Guild's Executive Board meetings. He also recommended me for ASC membership.

After your filming, did you continue to work on the film?

On occasions, I would take my footage and screen it for Antonioni. His reactions were subtle, a simple nod or slight shaking of his head. That was more than a thousand words from him. I recognized what he liked and did not like. In the end, several of my shots ended up in the movie, blending into the scene of the student outbursts. During the last month of production, since my documentary assignment was over, I was asked to continue as production still photographer for Bruce Davidson (Magnum), who was leaving for another assignment. This new assignment became a precious opportunity to watch Antonioni work and take production stills of the protagonist (Mark Frechette) landing his airplane and being consequently shot by the police. Antonioni–I was told by his personal assistant Rina Macrelli that it is his daily routine–asked the crew to step aside and give him a moment to prepare the scene alone; no questions, no interference. I read later in an interview Antonioni gave (The Architecture of Vision) that he never prepared himself the night before. He knew the script inside and out. But he needed to see each location or set with a fresh eye to form a visual construct of the scene, only then did the staging proceed; actors and camera were choreographed after seeing the surroundings, the environment in which the drama unfolds and action takes place. I understood then Antonioni's perceptual stance: one eye open to the outside and one eye turned toward the inside. Watching him work was an invaluable experience in the early stage of my career.

You also appear in Zabriskie Point*'s last airport scene as a photographer, right?*

While I was taking stills, Antonioni told me to be in the scene as a news photographer mixed in with the other extras. I was already dressed like one and carried a few cameras around my neck; I jumped in without hesitation. I was a bit stiff at first and he told me I should move like an excited, intense newspaper photographer! He did not miss a beat. A crucial lesson from Antonioni's approach to filmmaking is that one needs to see beyond what one has already seen and beyond what one wants to see. From the single opportunity to shoot the screen test to the rare chance to be immersed in the storm of demonstrations sweeping America in the late sixties, I gained a wealth of insight into filmmaking. Besides, I developed a network of professional and personal friendships that have enormously enriched my life.

The film ends with one of the most evocative sequences in the entire history of cinema, I am referring to the famous explosion: shot with seventeen cameras - conceived in an atmosphere of absolute visual rarefaction and declined in a hypnotic space-time suspension - it is undoubtedly one of the cinematographic icons of the entire twentieth century. What do you remember?

Unquestionably the final sequence is phenomenal; the dream-like images transcend the visual story telling. The house explosion in Arizona was the work of the main unit and the slow-motion explosion of the selected household and food items was carried out by the special effects unit. While I was in Los Angeles, I visited the special effects set on MGM lot where the crew was filming the explosion against the tall painted sky-blue wall. Surrounded by stacks of hay to prevent the debris from scattering all over, the items to be exploded were placed in air-compressed canisters. No dynamite was used. On cue they were released and captured on highspeed cameras. One camera assistant mentioned 400 frames per second in his camera, but I am not certain of others. And other specifics escape me now, but as I understood they repeated the process for a few days. Prior to the explosion I was given a list of images depicting the snapshots of American life; supermarket, hair saloon, oil field, car sale lots, etc., nearly a hundred snapshots of Americana. These were to be superimposed over air raids and combined with Daria's illusive vision, imagination, of the house exploding. After filming an oil field in southern California my assignment was abruptly cancelled due to, I was told, the studio's concern over the California government's scrutiny of the script. To avoid further political pressure, I think Antonioni's alternative solution was a brilliant and powerful one; extracting the symbols of American possession and obsession, annihilating them in a dream-like sequence. As I watched it with Pink Floyd's score, the experience was sublime.

What can you tell me about the Italian cinematographer Alfio Contini AIC?

Alfio Contini was a friendly, approachable man. He made helpful comments when he saw my footage, translated by Macrelli.

Director Michelangelo Antonioni and cinematographer Alfio Contini on the set of *Zabriskie Point* (1969). Photo by Hiro Narita

hiro narita. depth of field

I remember he and his crew from Italy rented apartments near Hollywood Blvd and cooked their meals together in the evenings. He invited me once but I missed the opportunity because I was moving around. I was sorry I did not have the time to meet him socially and chat. Importantly, I wish I understood the conversations between Antonioni and Contini on the sets. Did they talk in a unique code only artists can communicate with, or how much or how little did Antonioni verbalize his ideas to Contini? Only the subtle body language between them remains in my memory. I learned later that Contini photographed *Il sorpasso (1962)*. I thought it a fantastic movie; dynamic, elegant and very contemporary even today. I can only imagine that Contini's creative energy was bursting out under his gentle demeanor.

You mentioned Il sorpasso, *directed by Dino Risi. The film is considered as a precursor to the road movie. In the USA it was released under the title* The Easy Life. *It is said to have inspired in a sense* Easy Rider *(1969) by Dennis Hopper. Did you know the film then? Did you see it at the time?*

The film was recommended to me by my friend Walter Donati in Italy several years ago and he mentioned that it inspired Dennis Hopper's *Easy Rider*. After seeing *Il sorpasso* for the first time, I was convinced that the film was a harbinger of road pictures, and I definitely saw its mark on *Easy Rider*. Besides, I was impressed by Vittorio Gassman's and Jean-Louis Trintignant's virtuoso tragi-comedy performances. Fifty years later, the film remains relevant and invigorating. I read that it was one of the most popular and successful Italian films of that year, and I can see why. Alfio Contini's work is forever preserved and memorialized in the film.

In the 1970s, Daria Halprin developed an interest in creative arts therapy. In 1978, she and her mother Anna founded the Tamalpa Institute, which is based not far from your residence. Have you seen Daria again?

I saw Daria Halprin a few times during *Zabriskie Point*, and I met her again almost fifty years later when Donati and documentary filmmaker Veit Bastian asked me to introduce them to her. I knew where her Tamalpa Institute (creative arts and dance therapy) was situated and took the chance to hand-deliver my letter of introduction. As I parked my car across the street from the institute office, I saw a woman exiting the building and I recognized it was Halprin. I shouted, "Daria!" She wore a puzzled expression at first but soon she recognized me and I quickly presented my letter and we exchanged our fond memories of *Zabriskie Point* on the street. Ever since, I have been a supporter of her Institute and we make a point of having lunch in the neighborhood once a year.

Did you meet Dean Tavouralis, the film's production designer and future Oscar winner for The Godfather Part II *(1974), directed by Francis Ford Coppola? Tavouralis was on his first film in fact ...*

I am very fortunate to have known Dean Tavouralis and his brother Alex, also an artist. He said in an interview years later, "...the décor should advance the story. But to the eye it should be invisible...to the mind it should speak." I love his philosophy. His notions are embodied in his superb production designs, a textbook for filmmakers both esthetically and conceptually.

Did you meet the director Michelangelo Antonioni again after your experience on Zabriskie Point?

After *Zabriskie Point*, I did not see Antonioni for about a dozen years. My wife and I literally bumped into him and his wife, Enrica Fico, on a street in Lido di Venezia, where we were attending the Venice Film Festival and *Never Cry Wolf* was shown in its programs. Antonioni said he was there not for the film festival but for the Biennale, which was exhibiting some of his paintings. We immediately went to see the exhibits. Another occasion came later at the Pacific Film Archive in Berkeley after Antonioni received the Academy Honorary Award.

hiro narita. depth of field

Hiro Narita and Michelangelo Antonioni at Pacific Film Archive, Berkeley, California. He received an honorary Oscar a week earlier in Hollywood

What do you remember about that exhibition? What was Michelangelo Antonioni like as a painter?

His paintings were not architectural and exact as I envisioned and saw in his movies. They were fascinating abstractions of landscapes; gentle colors and textures that were more organic than geological. I read that Antonioni accidentally saw that motif when he was putting together bits and pieces of one of his old paintings that had been shredded. Often, he would start with a small painting, photograph it and enlarge it, transforming the microscopic into the macroscopic, revealing the previously unseen, and, in the process, exposing the complexity behind the ordinary. *Zabriskie Point*, a case in point, takes on a certain explosive shape and dimension beyond the images.

Did you do an internship with John Korty and Victor J. Kemper on Michael Ritchie's The Candidate *(1972), starring Robert Redford in the role of the young lawyer Bill McKay who is persuaded to run as a Democratic Party candidate in the Senate election?*

documentary to narrative

After I completed my apprenticeship with Korty, I worked as a freelance cameraman whenever opportunities knocked on my door while continuing my practice as a graphic designer. When Korty was hired to film the second unit of *The Candidate*, the parade and a few other scenes with Robert Redford, he asked me to operate an additional camera. The shoot was more like a documentary; spontaneity was the key. After the film I met Redford again when Carroll Ballard and I were invited to the Sundance summer workshop comingling with many filmmakers and prominent actors. It was an exciting event, furthering my understanding of filmmaking.

John Korty is the director of The Autobiography of Miss Jane Pittman *and the documentary* Who Are the De Bolts? And Where Did They Get Nineteen Kids? *(Academy Award for Best Documentary Feature) and he took you under his wing. With him, you collaborated as an assistant cameraman, gaffer, projectionist, film-poster designer, cinematographer, in your first movies such as* Riverrun *(1968) as assistant camera,* Silence *(1974) as cinematographer.*

I first met Korty at the San Francisco Art Institute when he gave a talk on occasion to Graphic Design students. Then I met him again at the design studio where he hired me as a production assistant. Upon returning from the Army in 1966, I reconnected with Korty and began my apprenticeship at Stinson Beach for the next three years. With my renewed interest in filmmaking, I trained in many facets of film production, including animation. Korty had just completed *Funnyman* with Peter Bonerz (*Medium Cool*), and he was preparing for *Riverrun* for which he was director/cameraman and I became an assistant cameraman, a gaffer, and all-around production assistant. At the time, his naturalistic approach required few lights, so I was able to cover the two roles without over-extending myself. In fact, there were only half a dozen of us in the entire crew, some doubling roles. The experience for me was like an on-the-job training no film school could have provided.

hiro narita. depth of field

Silence *(1974) was your first movie as cinematographer...*

After the film's completion Korty relocated his studio to American Zoetrope briefly, then to Mill Valley, a town just north of San Francisco, and I too moved to a small town nearby. As I ventured out as a freelance cameraman, Korty hired me on *Silence*, a film about a deaf child's adventure in a forest. Will Geer (*Jeremiah Johnson*) in a hermit role and his extended acting family members took part in the film. Shot almost entirely outdoors, it was my very first feature film, a safe entry into the full-length narrative genre. Surrounded by young beginners like myself, our energy and enthusiasm held it together in more ways than one.

What can you tell me about Vegetable Soup *- 78-part educational children's program (1975-78, for PBS-tv)? Did your friend Korty also work as animator on this program?*

Produced by the Public Broadcasting Service, this educational series included short live actions and animations subcontracted to filmmakers throughout the country. I directed several episodes

Vegetable Soup. Hiro Narita, Barbara Parker Narita, William Smock behind the camera and Thomas Martin. Courtesy of Pictures & Words

through my studio (Pictures & Words). They were about different ethnic children sharing their particular tradition at home, different food, and activities; understanding and taking part in the uniqueness of their customs and cultures. Separate from mine, Korty Films directed many episodes, including animation. Such a series provided great opportunities for up-and-coming filmmakers and I truly valued these publicly-funded programs. Incidentally, the girl I cast in one of my films ended up as a young lead in *Farewell to Manzanar* shortly after.

He Is My Brother *is a 1975 American drama film directed by Edward Dmytryk. He was known for his 1940s noir films and received an Oscar nomination for Best Director for* Crossfire *(1947). Also worth mentioning are other films such as* The Caine Mutiny *(1954) and* The Carpetbaggers *(1964). What do you remember about your collaboration with Dmytryk?*

The fictional story of a young shipwreck survivor meets a native girl on a Hawaiian Island, where Father Demien (a real late 19th century figure) cared for the victims of leprosy; it is a love story against a historical background. When I met director Edward Dmytryk (*The Cain Mutiny*), well-respected director and later a professor of film theory at a university, I was unaware of the Hollywood director's working method or system, even that there was such thing in practice or that it existed. My limited working relationship with directors so far had been open and collaborative. On the set of *He Is My Brother* Dmytryk held absolute control of camera angles, focal length of lens, even camera heights, and, of course, the actors; except the lighting. Having being a film editor prior to becoming a director, he was very sure about the essential elements required to create a scene, and, due perhaps to scheduling and budgetary constraints, he proceeded to direct the film he had already set in his mind as proficiently as possible. He did not need any suggestions from me, and I felt somehow uninvolved. Perhaps I was naïve and, in his eye, very much a novice. As I gained more experience and worked with different directors, I came to understand each director's own forte and I had to adapt my working relationship accordingly.

With Korty you collaborated again for a TV movie called Farewell to Manzanar *(1976) for which you received your first Primetime*

Jeanne Wakatsuki Houston, coauthor of the book and screenplay, during *Farewell to Manzanar* filming. Photo by Barbara Parker Narita

documentary to narrative

Emmy Awards nomination. The movie is based on the book of the same name published in 1973 by Jeanne Wakatsuki Houston and James D. Houston. The book describes the experiences of Jeanne Wakatsuki and her family before, during, and following their relocation to the Manzanar concentration camp due to the United States government's internment of Japanese Americans during World War II.

Upon Korty's commitment to direct *Farewell to Manzanar* (Universal Television) he took a big chance in hiring me as director of photography, my very first major project. He felt the story was pertinent to me as a Japanese American citizen. Based on a real family experience, it dealt with the controversial subject of Japanese-American internment during World War II; a taboo subject rarely mentioned publicly, even among Japanese American themselves. The historical event was buried, if not reduced to a few descriptions in text books. I had to admit I knew very little about it myself as an immigrant from Japan in 1957, and I had to educate myself on the subject quickly.

How did you do the research and preparation work?

To prepare ourselves Korty and I studied the photographs taken by Dorothea Lang and Ansel Adams for the War Relocation Authority, absorbing the mood and the atmosphere in which the people endured their incarceration. Although their photographs depicting the internees' harsh and bleak living conditions were censored by the US government till decades later, we were able to draw on the stark reality of their tragic lives as depicted in the story.

Where and how did the filming take place?

The prologue, the present-day family's homage to the former Manzanar camp, now a memorial site and a ghostly shadow of the past, was filmed in Manzanar. It is a desert town north-east

Farewell to Manzanar: John Korty and Stewart Barbee (2nd assistant camera).
Photo by Barbara Parker Narita

Farewell to Manzanar: filming at the Tule Lake camp site.
Photo by Barbara Parker Narita

Farewell to Manzanar. Photo by Barbara Parker Narita

Farewell to Manzanar. Photo by Barbara Parker Narita

Farewell to Manzanar

Farewell to Manzanar's promotional brochure designed by Hiro Narita

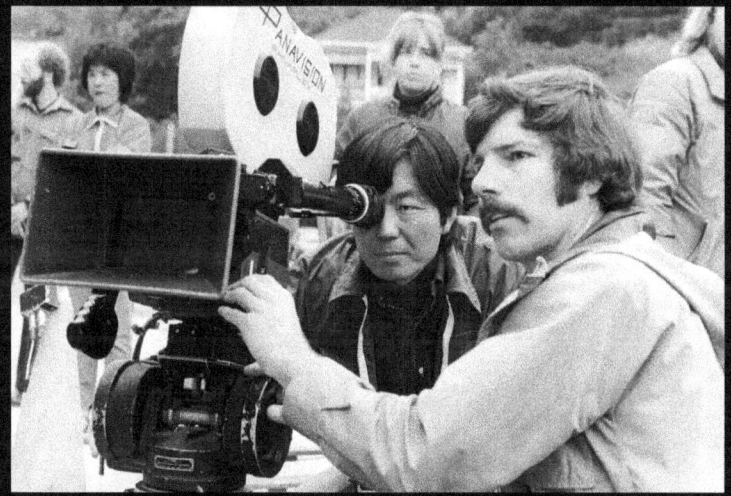
Farewell to Manzanar: Hiro Narita, Barney Colangelo (1st assistant camera) and behind Narita is Aggie Rodgers (costume designer)

hiro narita. depth of field

Farewell to Manzanar: filming for the scene in which Ko Wakatsuki (played by Yuki Shimoda) joins his family when he arrives at Manzanar after his detention at a Justice Department site. Photo by Barbara Parker Narita

of Los Angeles. But the core of family life in the camp was filmed at Tule Lake, California, almost 500 miles north of Manzanar. Tule Lake was another internment camp site with some remnants still standing, and we build our barrack sets reclaiming several old ones. When the production began, word spread and many former internees, their family and friends volunteered as set builders, prop makers, and extras in the film. The film became a community project. My wife also volunteered in recruiting extras and taking production stills. It became an important experience for me both professionally and personally; developing my skill and understanding Japanese-American history that I might have overlooked.

Do you remember an intense moment during the making?

Actor Yuki Shimoda (*Pacific Overture*) who played Jeanne's father was actually incarcerated at Tule Lake camp as a young man. One intense scene in which he arrives at the camp after being released from a prison was unrehearsed. Kory wanted to capture Shimoda's raw reaction to reuniting with his family and facing the bleak reality of the camp he actually experienced in his youth. Korty felt Shimoda's accute memory of the past might spontaneously resurface and he did not want to see that naked moment till the camera rolled. Thinking back, it is possible that Shimoda himself did not want to rehearse the scene. His performance was priceless. We shot the scene as if it was a real event.

Which sequence did you like the most?

There is a night riot scene, an uprising organized by dissenting internees refusing to sign the loyalty oath to the United States. The ideal location turned out to be in a minimum-security prison yard (partially defunct then) east of San Francisco. There I set up two 12-foot scaffoldings–we did not build guard towers–behind the approaching rioters. On top of them I placed roving spot lights simulating search lights. Many rioters carried flame torches and, essentially, that was the lighting I relied on. Against the black sky, the dust kicked up by the bellowing rioters and the whirling smoke from the torches intensified the sense of turbulence; a heighten realism. Besides, they helped obscure the unwanted present-day street lights in the distant background. I was very happy with the outcome. In other projects years later, I applied this approach; relying on bare essentials and achieving more than I could have imagined.

The film also stars the actor Pat Morita. What role did he have in the film? What do you remember about him? Pat Morita was nominated for the 1984 Academy Award for Best Supporting Actor for his portrayal of Mr. Miyagi in The Karate Kid *directed by John G. Avildsen.*

Added to the cast were a number of accomplished Japanese American actors; Pat Morita (*The Karate Kid*) and Mako (*The Sand Pebbles*). Morita portrayed a photographer loosely modeled on Tobo Miyatake, a professional photographer who was also incarcerated at the Manzanar camp. He smuggled in a lens and built a wooden camera to document camp life; his photographs remain as important historical records of the incident. Morita in his career was

Actor Pat Morita in *Farewell to Manzanar*. Photo by Barbara Parker Narita

documentary to narrative

a recognized actor/comedian before becoming a household name with the success of *The Karate Kid*. But during our filming he seemed very private and reticent, unlike other comedic roles he played in the past. Perhaps he retained his character role on and off camera. His role was small, but he left a memorable presence in the film.

Did you meet Jeanne Wakatsuki Houston and James D. Houston while filming Farewell to Manzanar?

As script writers both Jeanne and James Houston often visited us on locations, and their children too joined in making props and helped with various chores. Jeanne must have stayed for a while at the Tule Lake location because she was a friendly fixture on the set and I got to know her well. And she was a valuable and direct source of information when Korty needed it. I met the Houstons again at the 25th anniversary of the film with many actors present, but by the 45th anniversary held on Zoom last year there were only a half dozen of us left.

In Farewell to Manzanar *you also edited the brochure of the film...*

Korty wanted to share the memorable experience of making the film with the cast and crew and he thought of a simple photo album with their credits: a commemorative gift to them as his appreciation. He asked me to design it and the result was the brochure. I came up with a simple, graphic barbed wire above the title; I thought it captured the internment camp that held captive the people and their life during the war. I picked the earthy, brown paper to remind them of the desolate desert.

Do you want to remember a curiosity about Farewell to Manzanar?

Here is an interesting side story; a karma, another coincidence. During *Zabriskie Point*, when I was not filming riots or demonstrations, Antonioni sent me to Tule Lake to film the remains of the wartime internment barracks, some completely collapsed and in decay, others converted to duck-hunting lodges. I knew little of the significance of such buildings, nor the place, let alone about the relocation of 120,000 Japanese Americans during the war. And why was Antonioni interested in the place and what was the connection to *Zabriskie Point*? As I was discreetly setting up my camera, a young boy about 10 years old, who was playing alone with broken pieces of the barracks, approached me and quite innocently said, "You know, Japs used to live here". I wondered what and how much his parents told him of the place he lived in and called his home. Six years later, it was at the very same location, almost the same spot, where we built the set of *Farewell to Manzanar*! Antonioni's curiosity still remains a mystery to me today. I feel now as if I had been thrown into a psychic space and time where people and events gravitate toward each other and crisscross, eluding our own recognition.

Later you worked with Korty again two more times.

Through the years Korty mentored many aspiring filmmakers who later excelled in their careers. And I had other opportunities to film his TV movies: *Children of The Mist* with Vanessa Redgrave and *The Hunting Passion* with Jane Seymour, as well as documentaries.

About Children of The Mist *also known as* They, *what can you tell me and what do you remember about Redgrave?*

With *Children of The Mist* (based on Rudyard Kipling's short story) I had an interesting insight into how an actor coped with movie sets crowded with gears in constant rearrangement. I am sure every actor has his or her own way of dealing with it. I tried my best to be as unobtrusive as possible and asked of my crew to do the same during set-ups, not disrupting the actors' train of thought. Usually, they disappeared from the set, avoiding being

documentary to narrative

Farewell to Manzanar: Hiro Narita and director John Korty

John Korty at the center surrounded by his former mentees (2019)

hiro narita. depth of field

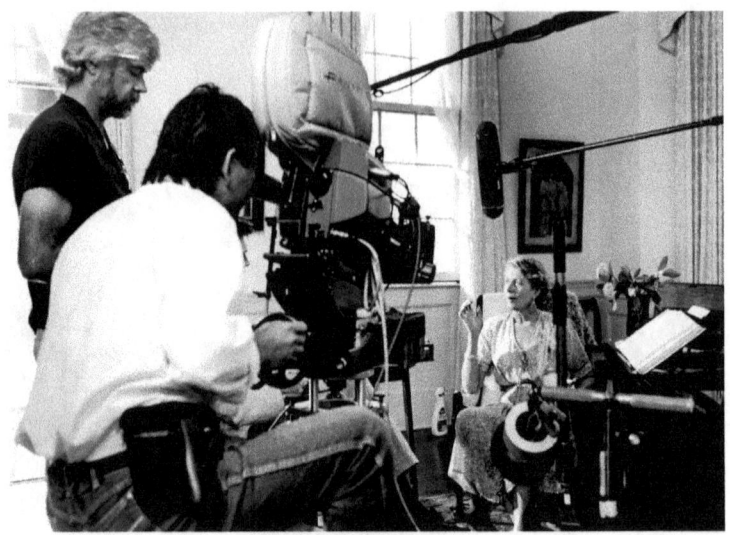

They / Children of Mist: Hiro Narita and Vanessa Redgrave
with camera assistant Rob Morey

in the way of the crew. During those moments, Redgrave was often in my sight; rather than stepping out, she remained on the set or in the vicinity of the set, seemingly unaffected by the hectic buzz. I gauged she was simply accustomed to it or had trained herself to shut out the peripheral activities. But after a while, I began to sense that she had an innate ability to be alone in a crowd, protected by invisible walls, retreating into her private space. Her self-control was different from "getting accustomed to" or "ignoring it". I think she developed and carried with her this secure world she could retreat to whenever and wherever she wanted it; seeing but not taking notice at the same time. At least this was my way of observation. Redgrave's effortless presence on the set, in turn, made our work feel less evasive and helped generate mutual courtesy.

Did you collaborate on the film Who'll Stop the Rain *(1978) directed by Karel Reisz and starring Nick Nolte, with cinematography by Richard H. Kline? If so, in what role?*

documentary to narrative

I did a few additional shots for the film directed by Steven C. Jafee, son of producer Herb Jafee. It was a very simple and brief work over the Golden Gate Bridge. So I did not meet with Richard Kline. However, Jafee and I were reunited years later on *Star Trek VI: The Undiscovered Country*, which Jafee produced and Nicholas Meyer directed.

The Last Waltz was a concert by the Canadian-American rock group The Band. The event was filmed by director Martin Scorsese and made into a documentary of the same title in 1978. In this documentary you collaborated as additional cinematographer. Martin Scorsese is one of the greatest American directors: he has signed masterpieces such as Taxi Driver *(1976),* Raging Bull *(1980),* Goodfellas *(1990). How did you become part of his project?*

The Last Waltz took place at Bill Graham's Winterland Ballroom in San Francisco, celebrating The Band's last concert, and it was an extraordinary experience for me. David Myers, an accomplished documentary and narrative cameraman (*Woodstock, Welcome to LA*) and already a hired member of the project, convinced Martin Scorsese to add me to the roster of additional directors of photography.

How did you prepare for such an event?

In the preproduction meeting, Scorsese gave each cameraman a massive shooting script with detailed camera instructions for practically every line of the lyrics in every song; which camera to focus on who, wide or close-up, etc. I was awestruck by the extensive preparation and previsualization Scorsese did prior to the concert. We were also given headsets so we could hear his direction during the shoot. Michael Chapman was in charge of the stage lighting, cameras were positioned on each side of the stage, two in front among the audience;, Myers had a hand-held roaming camera on the stage; and finally myself in the backstage looking toward the audience. Myers told me before the concert began, with a subtle rolling of his eyes, "Go with your instincts", in spite of the detailed shooting script. Sure enough, once the stage exploded with music and a bonanza of lights flashing, I was thrown into a pandemonium. I could barely understand what Scorsese was screaming into our headsets. Although I had a production assistant who followed the script and shouted to me which singer or instrumentalist I should catch at the given moment, I struggled, not having the best angles, and aimed my camera at whatever seemed right, under such hopeless circumstances.

You worked among others with cinematographers of the importance of László Kovács HSC-ASC and Vilmos Zsigmond HSC-ASC, both born in Hungary. They had previously worked in cult films such as Easy Rider *(Kovács) and* Close Encounters of the Third Kind *(Zsigmond). What do you remember about them?*

At the time, I knew them only by their names and their outstanding work. We were introduced to each other–I was in great awe at meeting them–at the preproduction meeting, but never had further talk with either of them. Eight years later, finally, I met and talked with László Kovács when he was filming *Crackers* for Louis Malle in San Francisco, and he asked me to shoot a few additional shots of a meter maid in action in the Mission district. And while I was filming *James and Giant Peach,* he was filming *Copy Cat* next to our studio and invited me to the set. Kovács was generous and gave me a tour of the set, explaining the complex lighting he was dealing with. With Zigmond I worked on another concert film *The Rust Never Sleep* directed by Neil Young, and in 2006 I went to hear his talk on *The Black Dahlia* at Sonoma International film Festival. There I finally had an informal conversation with him and I found him very friendly, just as Kovács was.

Was there a particular moment that you remember pleasantly?

documentary to narrative

There were some memorable moments from my camera positions that no one, Scorsese included, could have envisioned in the middle of the live frenzy of the concert. In one of those moments, I saw Levon Helm through a gap between the musicians. While drumming, Helm had a long singing solo, his face in profile right against the mic to his right. The spotlight from the second floor cast him in a strong backlight. I felt I should stay on him as long as I could, and I did. Such was the instinctive moment Myer advocated.

In The Last Waltz *there are musical icons like Neil Young, Van Morrison, Neil Diamond, Bob Dylan, Joni Mitchell, Eric Clapton. Did you get to know them? Were you a fan of their music?*

I had been a fan of Neil Young and Joni Mitchell before the concert. But during the filming of *The Last Waltz*, it was impossible to meet with any musician, as you can imagine the chaotic situations.

In Apocalypse Now (1979), epic psychological war film directed and produced by Francis Ford Coppola, with legendary actors like Marlon Brando, Robert Duvall, Martin Sheen, Dennis Hopper, you collaborated as an additional camera operator. How did you get contacted?

Second unit director/cinematographer Stephen H. Burum–I think he did additional work on *Black Stallion* and heard about me through the grapevine–contacted me to operate camera for the additional shoot at Coppola's property. He had already done an extensive 2nd unit job in the Philippines and he was very familiar with film.

Can you tell me in detail about your work in the film?

My experience on *Apocalypse Now* was sporadic and minor, operating camera for Caleb Deschanel and Stephen H. Burum: close-ups of Willard's dossier, bullets hitting the boat, etc. that the editors needed to punctuate and weave the scenes. Deschanel asked me to film the closeup of Martin Sheen's head rising bove the river's surface, only then Francis Coppola was present. We filmed these toward the end of the post-production at Coppola's vineyard and a nearby river. I remember seeing a young boy, Charlie Sheen, accompanying his father and nonchalantly watching him work. Little did I know we would be working together in the future.

So you worked with both Burum and Deschanel? Separately obviously?

The work with Deschanel came at a different time, maybe after Burum. For some of the shots, Deschanel had to match Vittorio Storaro's lighting and I am sure he studied the edited scenes before our work.

The image of Sheen emerging from the river is one of the most iconic in the film...

I am not certain if it was a reshoot or an added shot to the scene. But Deschanel knew the exact lighting required for the image. My wife was there as script supervisor, so the timing of Sheen's emergence must have been equally a key element of the shot. As I mentioned before it was the only time Coppola was present to direct the additional shoot.

As we will find out later, your wife Barbara also worked in the film industry. She worked then on Apocalypse Now. *How did she get involved in the film?*

In the final editing stage of *Apocalypse Now*, Barbara was hired to reconstruct and generate a script updated from the edited version, since the film had gone through many changes. She mentioned that the editors worked around the clock in a frantic atmosphere, with the release date approaching. The final script–for the archives–needed to reflect the exact dialogue and the action changes true to the final-cut of the movie.

documentary to narrative

Apocalypse Now *is a magnificent film: Vittorio Storaro AIC-ASC won the Oscar for best cinematography, his work was incredible, do you agree?*

Storaro's fluid camera work and the images of the intense battle scenes enhanced realism, crossing the threshold of surrealism. With his dramatic lighting Brando's character became a profoundly mythical figure. As witnessed in much of Storaro's work in collaboration with Bernardo Bertolucci and later with Carlos Saura, his exploration into color deepened and proliferated in *Apocalypse Now*, adding another depth to our visual experience. I believe his work on the movie is truly a great achievement in cinema history.

Apocalypse Now *was your classmate Richard Beggs' first film: he won an Academy Award for Best Sound for this film.*

I wondered how Richard Beggs' background in painting developed his keen sense of sound and music. We have by convention assumed that picture and sound are not synonymous forms of expression. I realize now that his visual sensitivity was dominant at one point in his life but sound took over later in his career, though they stemmed from the same subconscious. In *Art & Physics*, surgeon Leonard Schlain explains that art interprets the invisible world and unites with physics in the higher realm of "universal mind" and true artists find the connection in all things–I would personally add mathematics here–intuitively. Artists' left and the right brain have freer traffic, constantly crisscrossing. So, according to Schlain's theory, painting and music are branches of the same tree: the mind. Beggs' transition to sound editing or design seems, in retrospect, organic and natural in his artistic capacity. I will ask him if he still paints today. Joni Mitchell is a great musician and a wonderful painter, as opposed to Beggs: but both are artists in in the truest sense.

The screenplay for the film, co-written by Coppola, John Milius, Michael Herr (narration), is loosely based on the 1899 novella Heart of Darkness *by Joseph Conrad. Did you know Conrad's novel?*

Joseph Conrad's *Heart of Darkness* was a reading requirement at the SF Institute, but I understood little of the core of the story at the time. The intensely realistic prose, coming to a head with an abstract, metaphysical framework, stays in my mind. I should read it again.

Coppola was one of the greatest exponents of New Hollywood, in general one of the most influential directors in the history of cinema. What do you think of his authorial poetics?

Film scholars and critic have written volumes on Coppola's life and his enormous creative faculty. Once, when I visited Eleanor, I saw him concocting a liquor, a new product, adding to his brand of wines. At another time, he told me of a good, simple recipe for spaghetti con vongole, always with simple, easy-to-understand language. He was, Eleanor mentioned, also editing a script at the time. So much of his vast literary knowledge and his grand vision are veiled under his façade, undetectable; he is as lucid as he is mystifying.

Did you see the premiere of the film when it was released in the US?

My wife and I saw the first cut together in San Francisco. And I was overwhelmed by its grandeur and beauty. I believe the version included the French plantation sequence–nearly half an hour long–which was taken out in the general release but restored in the director's cut.

More American Graffiti *is a 1979 American coming-of-age comedy film written and directed by Bill L. Norton. It is the sequel to the 1973 film* American Graffiti *directed by George Lucas. In this*

documentary to narrative

movie you were the camera operator, the cinematographer was Caleb Deschanel ASC. What memory do you have of the sixties that are told in the movie?

The success of *American Graffiti* reunited all those young actors (minus Richard Dreyfuss), and their energy and enthusiasm were pervasive on the sets. Their changes of make-ups and costumes reflected the passage of time in the storyline. Filmed in four different formats–anamorphic, wide, academy, and super 16mm–each corresponding to the four main characters and their respective stories, Deschanel had a very demanding and bewildering job of dealing with the technical complexity and visual styles. Of the four segments, I enjoyed most the character Toad in Vietnam, played by Charles Martin Smith (*American Graffiti*, *Untouchable*). We filmed the segment in Super 16 often handheld or using Shakicam–I am not sure who invented it or named it–composed of two aluminum poles joined forming T and the camera is mounted at the end of the long bar. My arms absorbed some shocks as I balanced the camera and followed the action. It gave me freer and smoother camera movements than a handheld camera on my shoulder. The disadvantage was that I was blind to what camera was seeing since video-tap was not available. So, in general, we relied on wider lenses and guesswork. The Shakicam (aka Poorman's Steadicam), in spite of its limitations, was very effective for the battle scenes. As 2nd unit D.P. I filmed Toad's escape from Vietnam in the Golden Gate Park in San Francisco. And few years later, Smith and I worked together again on *Never Cry Wolf*; this time for ten months.

What do you remember about Ron Howard as Steve Bolander (and future director of many successful films) and Harrison Ford as Officer Bob Falfa?

One thing that drew my attention was that Howard (director, *Beautiful Mind*, *Da Vinci Code*) often stayed on set even when he was not in the scene. Out of curiosity, I asked him if he needed to rest somewhere more comfortable. He replied, he wanted to observe the shooting as much as possible. Now I understand why. Harrison Ford, in spite of the meteoric rise after *Star Wars*, or because of it, was reticent behind the camera, almost hiding from public view. I struck up a conversation with him about woodworking, as I knew he was once a self-taught carpenter. And he opened up and we chatted till it was his time to be in front of the camera.

Music again. You were in fact one of the cinematographers of the documentary Rust Never Sleeps *(1979) the Neil Young's concert performance at the Cow Palace (October 22, 1978) directed by Neil Young and the camera operator of the documentary* Shadows and Light *(1980) directed by Joni Mitchell on 1979 Joni Mitchell's historic tour backed by an all-star band of jazz-fusion musicians. Young, Mitchell and before The Band. What do you remember about these great musicians?*

David Myers recruited me again as one of several cinematographers. On this project I reminded myself of Myers's doctrine that a camera operator on concert films should interact with the music and the musician from the guts, with instincts. As an enthusiastic director, Neil Young told the camera operators to be like a cameraman filming live sports events, to follow the action and not lose it. I believe he meant it literally as well as metaphorically; follow the performer in concert with the music; don't just aim the camera in an erratic search.
Joni Michell was less vocal about the filming itself, leaving it to Myers and other cinematographers. But she created magical atmospheres embracing cinematographers to make them see and feel her music. I wished I had had a longer involvement in the project to immerse myself in her holistic world. I found both Young and Michell very accessible as persons, their music inspirational; they are true artists, in my sincere opinion.

Do you care about music?

documentary to narrative

I am an ordinary listener of music. I appreciate it just as I appreciate any form of artistic expression: painting, sculpture, even dance. When a music triggers emotion and finds a pathway to other senses in me, I picture composition, color, and the interaction of light and dark–seemingly unconnected by themselves–shaping into images I can relate to. Conversely, when I see striking images, they trigger melody.

What do you like in particular?

Nowadays a local classical music station is always on in my car with the volume down. It is just to fill in the air and block out traffic noises. If the station happens to play exotic Middle Eastern or flamenco music or Puccini's opera, I might turn up the volume. When we were young, my wife and I collected hundreds of cassettes and CDs of many varieties; the blues, the Beatles, Bach, Pakistani chants, and so on, but they eventually and unfortunately became ornaments in the book shelves. I had no particular favorite then, but I regret now that I gave them all away.

You met your future wife Barbara Parker, while she was working with the documentary division of Francis Ford Coppola's American Zoetrope Studios. She also signed you on to shoot a short film.

Situated in a semi-industrial section of San Francisco, the original American Zoetrope offered office space to independent filmmakers. The lobby was open to all occupants and their associates. Like a utopian think-tank, filmmakers fraternized and shared their ideas and experiences, and pitched for work. Surrounding a large cappuccino machine and a billiard table, Coppola and Lucas too were often seen in the lobby chatting with them. This was a new film production base away from Hollywood. Barbara had her small office producing documentaries independently, not as a division of American Zoetrope. I frequented the studio looking for jobs as many aspiring people did as a matter of course, and Barbara learned that I had recently worked on *Zabriskie Point* as

hiro narita. depth of field

a documentary cameraman. She decided to hire me as one of the cameramen on her film about blues singers. I was still not confident of my career direction, mulling over my skill as a cinematographer, and I still practiced graphic design for a living. But when she saw my footage, she encouraged me to stay on course as cameraman. Our friendship developed as I found out she was very well-informed about Japanese cinema as well as classical literature.

Around this time, if I remember correctly, Lucas was finishing *THX1134* and gearing up for *American Graffiti* while Coppola was writing *The Godfather* script with Mario Puzo, posting 3x5 cards on his office walls. Lots of energy in the air. At one point I was hired to film screen tests of actors Coppola was considering for the film. He wanted cinema-verité coverages of the actors' impromptu rehearsals and interviews held in the screening room. The theater seats removed and a makeshift table and chairs in place, I lit the room broadly as I did not know what the actors were going to do. I filmed Coppola's stable of actors like James Caan and Robert Duvall. One night, Al Pacino arrived from New York with fashionably long hair. I heard that Eleanor Coppola cropped Pacino's hair short that night and he appeared as young Michael Corleone the next morning, visibly and strikingly transformed. And in the rehearsal Caan, Duvall, and Pacino established their connections right way, instinctively, I might add.

Great! Did you also film the audition of the legendary Marlon Brando? His portrayal of Don Vito Corleone is among the most iconic in the entire history of cinema.

During this period, I accompanied Coppola with a small crew to Maron Brando's home to film him testing for Don Corleone. Coppola said he needed to convince the studio executives of his choice of Brando. It was a clandestine mission and it was to be kept secret. I brought a 16mm Arri-BL, one umbrella light and a small unit to make the filming as simple and discreet as possible. Coppola brought his small video camera as well. At first,

Brando sat in front of a large mirror in the hallway, with wads of tissue in his mouth, pantomiming. He told us not to film this private moment. A short time later he said he was ready. Dressed in a dark suit, his hair tied tightly at the back, he held a cigar in one hand and a glass of wine in the other. Sitting on a couch he uttered muffled words gesturing as if he was talking to someone off camera–he did not want his voice recorded for this test because he had not settled on it. At one point the telephone rang, he picked it up casually, muffled a few words and hung up as if it was all part of the test. Then Coppola brought in Salvatore Corsitto, the actor to deliver the monologue in the beginning of the movie, and Brando simply listened. That was it. The test was over. In that short time, I saw Brando become the iconic Godfather. Ultimately, the production was based in New York and Gordon Willis did ground-breaking, beautiful work. Production designer Dean Tavouralis (*Zabriskie Point*) joined the team as production designer.

With what technical equipment did you shoot the auditions, in addition to the Arri you already mentioned??

I used a 16mm Arri BL for the interviews and rehearsal, and a Michell BNC 35mm camera for one scene between Al Pacino and Diane Keaton at the elegant Palace Hotel.

You were still young, you had not yet made your debut as a cinematographer. Was there no chance of participating in The Godfather, *as assistant cameraman or something similar?*

Without going into the complex industry practice, I can simply say that I could not work in New York or Hollywood at the time except on non-union movies, often labeled as runaway productions. *The Godfather* was produced by Paramount Pictures in New York, a signatory company to the International Alliance of Theatrical and Stage Employees. American Zoetrope on the other hand was subject only to San Francisco bylaws and as a member of the

Cinematographers' Guild under the San Francisco chapter and it allowed me to work on the screen test. Even after the Emmy nomination I received for *Farewell to Manzanar*, I could not work on so-called Hollywood or studio pictures under their jurisdiction. Citing the Taft-Hartley Act of the Federal Labor Law–I won't go into details–I warned the union in Los Angeles to accept me, otherwise I was prepared to file a lawsuit against them. And finally in 1987 I was placed on the Hollywood experience roster of the Motion Picture Association. It was a long, heart-wrenching process to overcome. On *Zabriskie Point*, for instance, Antonioni initially suggested I work as an additional camera operator but I was banned by the union in Los Angeles. For me to shoot the documentary, the producer found a loophole in the rules and made an arrangement to buy stock footage from me as if purchasing film from an independent source, thereby avoiding having me as a studio employee; a clever way to get around the union rules. The rules have been more lenient in recent years and those who can prove their qualification are accepted into as members, and after working over thirty days in a calendar year for a signatory company they are automatically placed on the Hollywood experience roster.

After the auditions you shot for Coppola, did you visit the set of The Godfather?

While the film was being shot in New York, I was busy building my own company with my wife and it did not occur to me to visit the *The Godfather* set.

You married to Barbara on 8 September in 1971?

By the time Coppola relocated American Zoetrope to the historic Sentinel Building in the heart of the city and Lucas to Marin County (creating ILM, Industrial Light and Magic) across the Golden Gate Bridge, Barbara and I were married in Hawaii in my mother's presence. We then formed a company called Pictures and

documentary to narrative

Words with a third partner in the Fisherman's Wharf area of the city. Barbara represented "Words". There we worked on a variety of projects: Oakland Museum's California Architecture History (a multi-screen slide presentation), Vegetable Soup, and *Isamu Noguchi: Stones and Paper* for American Masters series on PBS.

Was it your wife Barbara who introduced you to director / cinematographer Carroll Ballard for whom she worked as screenplay supervisor for Never Cry Wolf?

The main portion of *Black Stallion* was filmed (Caleb Deschanel, DP) in Sardinia, Italy. But the remaining parts were filmed on an Oregon coast and a race track in southern California. During this phase, Barbara was hired by Carroll Ballard as script supervisor till the film's completion.

Is it true that your first encounters with Ballard were purely social, animated by a shared love for carpentry? Crafting wooden cabinets has been one of your passions for more than 50 years, hasn't it?

While Ballard was editing *Black Stallion* at Lucas Films, Barbara introduced me to him, saying I would get along with him. In a rather casual encounter, we mostly talked about cabinet-making and woodworking, a passion both of us held. At first, I did not want to seem like someone seeking a job, nor did I want Barbara to lobby on my behalf. He showed me some scenes from *Black Stallion* in progress which I thought were magnificent. Later on, I finally saw his cabinets and furniture. I was astonished by his beautiful design and his masterful craftsmanship. Just as he was a consummate filmmaker, he was a superb artist. Our friendship grew along with his wife Christina, and all of us ended up working on *Never Cry Wolf*.

Indies to Studios

1980s-1990s

With the movie Never Cry Wolf *(1983) directed by Carroll Ballard you won the Boston Society of Film Critics Award and the National Society of Film Critics Award. The film is an adaptation of Farley Mowat's 1963 autobiography of the same name and stars Charles Martin Smith as a government biologist sent into the wilderness to study the caribou population, whose decline is believed to be caused by wolves, even though no one has seen a wolf kill a caribou. Brian Dennehy is also featured in the film.* Never Cry Wolf *is without a doubt one of your best works...*

I think over again my small adventures.
My Fears.
Those small ones that seemed so big.
For all the vital things
I had to get and to reach.
And yet there is only one great thing.
The only thing.
To live to see the great day that dawns
and the light that fills the world.

-Old Inuit Song
(*from the* Never Cry Wolf *ending)*

Ballard showed me Maxfield Parrish paintings before we left for the north and he said he wanted to capture the magical light of the Arctic summer. That was the starting point and he never mentioned Parrish again. The story involves vast landscapes, several kinds of animal, changeable weather, and diverse cultures. Reading the script, I imagined what it might look like. But I knew most preconceptions–even well-researched ones–spring from my own personal memories and experiences. So, I was ready and open to whatever was there, seeing and appreciating it in the unfamiliar light. And many surprises awaited me. Ballard, a superb cinematographer himself, wanted to explore relentlessly and surprise himself. He sometimes said, "I've run out of ideas. What else can we do?" He described the meaning of a scene first, then searched for images that both explicitly and implicitly supported his ideas. Crucially, he said that atmosphere and landscape are important elements in the story, relevant characters without dialogue. In the end, the so-called visual style grew out of what we saw and how we captured it. Dealing with the unpredictable weather and situations beyond our control became the norm. After five months roaming in Alaska, British Columbia, and Yukon Territory, Ballard said he did not have a movie, especially with the scene of wolves hunting the caribous. Besides, the temperature dropped and the Arri cameras ceased to function. We decided to pack up. So, the following year, we spent another five months crisscrossing the vast north under the long, low summer sun near the Arctic Circle; often filming from late afternoon till early morning and sleeping during the day. This time we were better prepared with camera equipment. As we worked from spring to late summer, from freezing to warm then to freezing again, we did not have to winterize the CM3s. An economic and practical solution was to make a camera blimp, made of padded fabric like a down jacket, to cover the camera body. And in the inner pockets we put hand-warmers when needed, keeping the camera's moving mechanisms above freezing temperature. Even the camera batteries were kept in insulated boxes for longer battery life. This time, in lieu of Arriflex, we brought Panavision cameras with internal heating system for the dialogue scenes. As in the previous year, Ballard wanted extensive use of telephoto lenses; namely, 300mm, 600mm, and 800mm, for their visual impact, if not out of necessity with animals at a distance. Also used were wide angle lenses to capture the vastness of the magnificent landscape, adding visual cadence to the telephoto images. Nearing the end of production, the chameleon-like weather forced us to shoot a scene in fog, and in snow, and finally in drizzle conditions as the weather did not give us enough time to complete it during the earlier two attempts; logistical planning could not dictate to nature.

At one point, Disney commented that my photography was slipping off its benchmark and wanted me to change. They said that I was not using enough fill light on Smith or even on the wolves. Ballard, thanks to his conviction, supported me till the very end of the filming. I think *Never Cry Wolf* was the most inspiring, and I might add, demanding project I had encountered. It was a test of our perseverance and, to a large extent, keeping our sanity intact. During the ten months in the north spread over two years, I became Ballard's apprentice, stirring up my own potential to surface and grow. For that very reason, to receive the awards was to honor Ballard's ceaseless pursuit of vision.

The director Carroll Ballard was chosen by Disney president Ron Miller, based on his work on The Black Stallion *(1979). French director Louis Malle was originally supposed to direct the film...*

Never Cry Wolf had an interesting beginning before it landed in Ballard's hands. Originally it was a New York-based independent project with Louis Malle (*Lacombe, Lucien*) as director, and the preproduction had already begun a few years earlier. For whatever reason, Malle moved on to another project, *Pretty Baby*. And the producer Lewis Allen (*Lord of the Flies, Fahrenheit 451*), brought it to Disney. Whether Ballard was attached to it on the strength of *Black Stallion* or president Miller himself chose Ballard as director is unclear to me; maybe more intricate circumstances were in play resulting in Ballard becoming the director of the film.

Never Cry Wolf was the first independent production to be released by the new Walt Disney Pictures label?

It was produced under Amarok Productions (wolf in Inuit language) but financed and distributed by Disney. Perhaps it was the first arrangement of this kind for Disney.

As mentioned, the movie stars Charles Martin Smith and Brian Dennehy: Smith did not just act, but wrote (the narration for the film) and contributed to the whole creative process. He would later become a director. What do you remember his performance?

During the production Charles Martin Smith became a close friend of Farley Mowat, the author of book *Never Cry Wolf*, and deeply committed himself to the project. As he had immersed himself in the character of Tyler, however fictionalized a version of Mowat he was, Smith lived in Tyler's body and soul so long in the vast north. He once said he did not have to act, but simply *be* Tyler. His words, borne of his own experience, naturally con-

Never Cry Wolf: Hiro Narita next to Éclair Cameflex CM3.
Photo by Barbara Parker Narita

hiro narita. depth of field

Never Cry Wolf: director Carroll Ballard and Barbara Parker Narita. First assistant camera Paul Marbury is in front of the camera. Photo by Hiro Narita.

tributed to the narration in the film. Smith was also a musician playing piano, guitar, drums, and even bassoon and, knowing his wide range of artistic skills, I was not at all surprised that he became a film director. And not long after *Never Cry Wolf* he directed another of Mowat's stories.

You mentioned that Smith and Farley Mowat became friends. How was your encounter with the famous Canadian ethologist, writer and environmentalist?

Farley Mowat was a spirited and audacious storyteller with gusto. I enjoyed listening to his stories, even his harsh encounters in the arctic sounded romantic and exciting. I could picture him traveling alone in the tundra or exchanging wild adventure stories with Inuit hunters.

Brian Dennehy (in the film he played Rosie, an eccentric bush pilot) came to fame in the role of villain sheriff Will Teasle in the film First Blood *(1982) directed by Ted Kotcheff. What do you remember about him?*

indies to studios

"Larger than life" is a description I can give of Brian Dennehy. Even on a frozen lake he seemed unscathed. During the second year of filming, Carroll Ballard invited Ken Kesey (author of *One Flew Over the Cuckoo's Nest)* to Alaska to write additional scenes. Dennehy immediately struck affinity with Kesey, and I

Never Cry Wolf: novelist Ken Kesey visiting location in British Colombia.
Photo by Barbara Parker Narita

heard they talked late into the night whenever possible. Dennehy, showing no sign of fatigue, was always ready for work the next day. Although one or two of Kesey's scenes survived the final cut, the indelible inspiration he left on Ballard, I believe, was clear. And Dennehy too must have been energized by Kesey's brief presence.

There is a sequence where Tyler falls through the lake ice, sinks like stone to the bottom under the weight of his full Arctic gear, and then shatters the ice with his shotgun, fortunately still in hand. How did you make this scene? Was it the most dangerous shot to do?

A wide range of ideas was proposed to make this sequence possible. In the end, Ballard and the special effects supervisor settled for a series of extraordinary setups to create and capture the scene. I need to explain in steps to make some sense, though I lost track of which order we filmed. The first shot, Tyler falling into the frozen lake, was him simply ducking out of the frame. It was filmed in Atlin, British Colombia, Canada. The next shot of Tyler (a photo double) sinking to the bottom of the lake was filmed in Lake Tahoe, California, by underwater cameraman Al Giddings (Abyss). When Tyler struggles to break the frozen surface with his rifle, it was filmed in a heated swimming pool in Juno, Alaska, photographed again by Giddings. The ice surface was made of epoxy resin–very convincing as real ice sheet–which I covered with a large silk to simulate the snow above and lit with 9-light Fay overhead providing a bright ambience. Back in Atlin we filmed Tyler breaking through the ice; this was a very risky and perilous shoot. In the snow-covered frozen lake (the ice was over a foot thick) the special effects crew built a passage platform under water from an entry hole to a roughly 4x8 foot hole nearby which was left overnight to freeze, then covered with a thin layer of snow blending with the lake's surface. Wearing a diver's dry suit under his costume, Smith entered the lake from the entry hole and proceeded to walk to the designated spot with the aid of divers, while breathing air from a scuba tank. And on cue, he pushed the rifle through the ice, and then he was hoisted up by the divers through the shattered hole as if climbing out of the frozen lake, gasping for air. We were able to film one take a day because the hole had to be refrozen overnight for another take. Besides, it was unsafe for Smith to do the scene twice in a day due to hypothermia–he looked ten years older than when he entered the icy water. So, we shot something else simple or the wolves in the afternoon. I remember shooting it a few times because the rifle did not come out where the camera was aiming, or perhaps Smith misjudged the spot in spite of the thin needle we put through the ice as target. The final wide shot of Smith crawling out to safety was filmed at yet another lake nearby.

How were the wolves that appear in the film found? I imagine that the production turned to instructors, to specialized companies?

The main pack of Arctic wolves–you have to keep them as a pack because they are tightly knit social animals–were brought from California. The pure breeds were difficult to train to perform specific actions needed in the film, and the trainers pulled them off one trick at a time patiently. To contain the wolves in a given area, concealed electric wire fences were built around them to prevent them from running off to the wilderness. For the scenes of the wolves hunting the caribous (they were actually a semi-domesticated herd that the natives leased from the Alaskan government) we brought another pack of grey wolves from Washington State. Being German shepherd hybrid, they took the trainers' command almost like trained dogs. They loved chasing the caribous but never attacked or caught up to them because the caribous ran faster. We also had another pack at one point, pure breeds of various colors, for certain images Ballard wanted to capture: the wild and untamed gaze in their eyes and their unique trot. Altogether we had three packs of wolves, each with its own trainers working in different times and situations.

hiro narita. depth of field

Never Cry Wolf was composer Mark Isham's first film. What can you tell me about his music?

I remember Ballard saying something to the effect that the music by the original composer was too ornate, too orchestral, and when he heard Isham's music–I am not sure how and where–he chose to make the switch. Isham's music, even to untrained ears like mine, gave a beautiful impressionistic undertone to the movie,

The director (future Oscar-winning for L.A. Confidential) Curtis Hanson also collaborated on the script. Did you know him?

Ballard kept revising the original script by Hanson and many writers were recruited in due course. After the first year of shooting, Ballard and I with our wives took a break at Desert Hot Springs, California. Resting in a pool and chatting, we noticed a man nearby listening to our conversation and after recognizing Ballard, he approached us and introduced himself as Curtis Hanson! A small world. Barbara and I politely excused ourselves and left the pool.

What can you tell me about the photographic style of the film?

Ballard and I never discussed any specific visual style, even though he showed me Maxfield Parrish's work at the very beginning. How we responded and captured the images unfolding in front of our eyes created a visual texture, and in the end, I think it became the visual style. I don't recall his using the term "visual tyle." Ballard had a unique way of seeing things; precise at times and impressionistic at others. He was always on the lookout, near and far. We took many hikes and covered a wide terrain seeking great camera angles. But I think we need to recognize that editing is a crucial part of shaping that "visual style" we often refer to. Ballard said at one point that half of any great film can be attributed to editing.

indies to studios

Never Cry Wolf: director Carroll Ballard waiting on caribous to return.
Photo by Barbara Parker Narita

As mentioned before, thanks to Never Cry Wolf *you won the National Society of Film Critics Award and the Boston Society of Film Critics Award (Best Cinematography). The first important awards of your career. What do you remember?*

I was delighted by the awards. But importantly, I am happy when my work takes off and lives a life of its own, and I can watch it as a viewer and say, it looks great, how did they capture them?

Once Ballard was chosen to direct the film, the protagonist (who at first should have been William Katt - best known as the star of the television series The Greatest American Hero) *was also changed. What do you know about this anecdote?*

I only knew of Charlie Martin Smith cast as Tyler. But I do recall his initial arrival at the location was delayed by a day or two for reasons I was not aware of. There must have been some complications that snagged him. So, Smith was flown in a helicopter to prevent any further delay and he was dropped off at a remote lo-

NSFC

THE NATIONAL SOCIETY OF FILM CRITICS

1983

Annual Award

Best Cinematography
HIRO NARITA

for

"Never Cry Wolf"

Jonathan Baumbach
CHAIRMAN

Certificate of Achievement, The National Society of Film Critics Award

cation we had set up. Already dressed as Tyler, he stepped off the helicopter, and at that very moment we saw a very large grizzly bear rising in the distance. We all cerebrated this as an auspicious start.

Can you confirm that the production of the film took place from 1980 to 1981?

The production took place from May through late September in 1980 and 1981; that is, five months each year.

Never Cry Wolf was the first Disney film ever entered at the Venice Film Festival (premiered on September 1, 1983). President of the jury of that edition was Bernardo Bertolucci, while among the members of the jury there was also the Japanese director Nagisa Oshima. You have already mentioned your encounter after Zabriskie Point *with Michelangelo Antonioni (awarded the Career Golden Lion): were there other encounters that you remember with pleasure?*

I had glimpses of Bertolucci and Oshima in the crowd during the festival. But at a dinner party my wife and I sat at the table across from Madame Kashiko Kawakita and her daughter (working as her personal assistant). Even with my limited knowledge of the Japanese cinema history I knew of her as a major mover in introducing Japanese movies to Europe such as Kurosawa's *Rashomon* at the Venice Film Festival in 1951. Dressed in her signature attire-kimono she was very gracious and open, and I was very honored to meet her and speak with her. She was quite curious to know how a Japanese cinematographer like myself ended up working on an American movie. Later I learned that Madame Kawakita had a life-long friendship with Donald Richie (*The Inland Sea*), whom she introduced to Yasujiro Ozu (*Tokyo Story, Late Autumn*).

How was the film received at Venice?

Never Cry Wolf: actor Charles Martin Smith, John Wardrow (photo and stunt double) and Barbara Parker Narita. Photo by Hiro Narita

At breakfast, producer Allen read a review by a French film critic and was chagrined that the critic brushed off the crucial point of the story: human interference with nature's balance in the wild arctic. He implied that the story seemed so removed from his intellectual and relevant concerns in modern society, despite acknowledging its beautiful production value. I remember feeling some incongruency in the critic's awareness.

Before moving on to the direction of feature films, Ballard worked as a second unit cinematographer in George Lucas' Star Wars (1977). Have you ever talked about it, did he ever tell you about that experience?

I knew about Ballard's work on the famous Cantina scene, but I had never heard him mention it in all the years I knew him. In fact, in our social gatherings we rarely talked about movies, and that, in a way, kept our long friendship till today.

In the end there were no simple answers.
No heroes, no villains. Only silence.

(Charles Martin Smith – Tyler from *Never Cry Wolf*)

With Carroll Ballard you worked again as additional photographer in the movie Nutcracker: The Motion *Picture (1986), cinematography by Stephen H. Burum ASC.*

When I returned from the project *Fire with Fire* in Canada, Ballard was filming additional scenes needed for *Nutcracker,* for which children's book illustrator Maurice Sendak (author, *Where the Wild Things Are*) designed the sets and the costumes. My wife was working for Ballard as inhouse production manager (his company was called Lone Wolf) and as script supervisor. Ballard asked me to shoot the title sequence with a Christmas tree adorned with toy Nutcrackers. I was happy to do it as it brought back memories of my graphic design days.

In The Right Stuff, *a 1983 American epic historical drama film written for the screen and directed by Philip Kaufman, based on the 1979 book of the same name by Tom Wolfe, you worked with the cinematographer Caleb Deschanel again. The movie was nominated for eight Oscars, four of which it won. Your wife Barbara worked on the movie as Mr. Kaufman's assistant. The movie therefore had an exceptional cast, consisting of Scott Glenn, Sam Shepard, Ed Harris, Dennis Quaid, Barbara Hershey. What do you remember about this film, the cast, the shooting?*

I operated an additional camera for Caleb Deschanel in the welcome-home-astronauts scene in the Cow Palace Event Center and the parade scene with the astronauts accompanied by their wives, both filmed in San Francisco (substituting Texas locations). Involving hundreds of extras, they were very complicated logistically, but Philip Kaufman pulled it off patiently, tenaciously.

hiro narita. depth of field

Barbara, working as Kaufman's personal assistant, managed a multitude of tasks he faced daily, aside from the production. She mentioned once that her role included maintaining and coordinating the actors' needs, sometimes their demands behind the camera, maneuvering and keeping the burden off Kaufman's shoulders. It must have been challenging with all those young rising actors discreetly jostling for his attention. On this film many local freelance visual effects people were recruited, making it one of the most successful and celebrated films made north of Hollywood.

In Return of the Jedi *(1983) – also known as* Star Wars: Episode VI - Return of the Jedi – *directed by Richard Marquand, you worked as additional cinematographer: what do you remember?*

By the time I was brought in, *Return of the Jedi* was nearly completed, but Richard Marquand needed some additional shots to thread the story. We went to Death Valley, not far from Zabriskie Point, to film a glass plate and other cutaways in which R2-

Hiro Narita filming *Return of the Jedi* in Death Valley

D2 and C-3PO travel to Jabba Palace. We built a large plywood box to house a VistaVision camera (8-perf large format) and the crew, with a glass plate-window facing Jabba Palace in the distant background, to be filled with a matte painting later. On the glass the matte painter meticulously blacked out the area to be replaced with the painting. We fastened the camera securely to the ground so that the slightest vibration would not affect the precise compositing of the visual elements. Then we filmed C-3PO and R2-D2 advancing toward the Palace seen through the clear area of the glass. C-3PO's metal outfit was worn by Anthony Daniels, the only actor contracted to wear it (not an easy task in Death Valley), but R2-D2 was a remote-controlled robot for this shoot. Unexpectedly the robot would go haywire when it picked up radio signals from military airplanes flying over us. Marquand, who was by then well-accustomed to the tedious and idiosyncratic process, was very composed. So was Lucas who had seen everything before. The process was time-consuming and painstaking, but it was magic when the layers of elements were assembled and screened.

What can you tell me about the impact on American culture of the famous Star Wars *saga created by George Lucas?*

This is a very big question and I don't know where to begin. To talk about Star Wars and Lucas' creativity in a simple, abbreviated term, I would borrow a view from Joseph Campbell (author, *The Power of Myth*). *Star Wars* reawakened the power of folklore and myth that was fading in our culture, in our generation. And consciously or not, Lucas filled the void with fantasies and images that resonated with our inherent yearning. And he rewarded them. In *Star Wars*, our past, present, and future merged into a deceptively accessible movie. Much was said of his trials and tribulations in the production and the many negative opinions surrounding his efforts. But Lucas held to his conviction. *Star Wars*' timely release and its success was a momentous triumph in American cinema.

hiro narita. depth of field

Had you already met Lucas during his experience on Return of the Jedi?

Lucas came to Death Valley with Marquand for the shoot as writer and producer. He was often around in the ILM building when I spent time with the visual effects unit on some pick-ups. Since I first met Lucas in the early 70s at American Zoetrope, my direct working relationship with him did not come till later, when I filmed Panasonic commercials shown exclusively in Japan. He appeared, surrounded by R2-D2, 3-CPO, and Chewbacca, for the THX sound system installed in the Panasonic television.

In Indiana Jones and the Temple of Doom *(1984) directed by Steven Spielberg, the second installment in the Indiana Jones franchise, starring Harrison Ford, did you collaborate as a second unit?*

With Dennis Muren in charge of the visual effects, this project included bits and pieces of images against blue-screen with Harrison Ford, Ke Huy Quan and other actors, and a scene where Ford awakens from a dream in a cave, surrounded by burning candles. Spielberg must have set up a dozen camera angles despite the short scene. Lucas peeked in at the set and said to him teasingly, "I'd do in one shot". Spielberg responded, "But, I am not you". A great friendship and rivalry were evident, in a very amicable way.

Was Douglas Slocombe, the film's cinematographer, also present?

No, he was not. As often was the case, my work took place long after the first unit's completion. There was a quick close up of Ford on horseback I had to match with Slocombe's shot against the sunny sky in north Africa. On the day of the shoot, it was overcast outside ILM and when I mentioned it to the producer he said, go ahead and film it. There were, he added, so many weather mismatches in Africa but nobody is going to notice. I am sure

Spielberg was well aware of the situation. Sure enough, in the final film - where you were carried away by the action and the quick editing and the final color grading by Slocombe-my worries were erased. By the way, Ford was not on horseback: actually, he was sitting on a crane and the camera was aiming just above his chest.

What is your memory of Harrison Ford, in one of his most famous roles?

Five years had passed since I worked with him on *More American Graffiti* and his popularity had soared even higher. But he had not changed that much in my view. The staff at ILM treated him with respect but without superfluous worship and we all avoided trivial conversation with him for his privacy.

Steven Spielberg is among the most successful directors in the history of cinema. What do you think is his greatest quality?

In the limited work experience I had with Spielberg, I can simply describe him as open, nimble, and, remarkably, a quick thinker. By that I mean, there seemed to be a multitude of ideas going though in his head at lighting speed, but he was never exasperated or short of energy.

Gordon Parks was the first African American to produce and direct major motion pictures. He is best known for having published his photographs in the famous US magazine Life *for twenty years, and for having directed* Shaft the detective *in 1971, one of the first films of Blaxploitation. What can you tell me about your meeting with him and about* Solomon Northup's Odyssey, *a 1984 American television film based on the 1853 autobiography* Twelve Years a Slave *by Solomon Northup directed by Parks himself?*

I was caught off guard when the producer of *Vegetable Soup* contacted me and said she was producing a project I would enjoy.

hiro narita. depth of field

Hiro Narita with director Gordon Parks

Solomon Northup's Odyssey, an *American Playhouse* series for Public Broadcasting Service (PBS), was to be directed by Gordon Parks, and to be filmed in 16mm; its location, Savannah, Georgia.

I guess you were happy to work with Parks?

Parks was a legend in many ways and I was more than ecstatic and honored to be asked. A Renaissance man whose photographs, movies, music, and literary works were so expansive they were beyond my grasp, yet he never liked the term in reference to himself. Seemingly made of steel, Parks was amiable and engaging to talk to and his directorial style was succinct and clear to follow. Never more than needed was said to the cast, crew, or anyone else for that matter, and he managed to keep his complex emotions beneath an austere façade with wry humor and wit. I tried my best to understand him and keep up with his step. The story is about a free black man captured and sold into slavery and his subsequent escape. Needless to say, Parks was very attentive to color, composition, and the visual texture–the locations in Savannah provided many–but he expounded on them placidly

indies to studios

and focused on the actors so that their raw emotional expressions surface involuntarily, unconditionally beyond technical performance. I realized that from decades of photographing the civil rights movement, African American lives, and people in despair or in power, Parks' intuition to capture them was truly profound. And in this small budget period drama, finding and relying on the natural source of light, thereby minimizing the amount of movie equipment, was reassuring in my work. My wife was also working as script supervisor and we both became good friends with Parks till his passing.

In 2013, 12 Years a Slave *was released, directed by Steve McQueen. This film is also based on the same book by Northup and won the Academy Award for Best Picture. You have surely seen it. Did it remind you of your work with Parks?*

Yes, I recognized many images, even the dialogues in McQueen's version; they were, however, much bigger in scale and in production value. I thought the film was excellent and skillfully made.

And what can you tell me about the documentary Half Past Autumn: The Life and Works of Gordon Parks *(2000) directed by Craig Rice?*

Half Past Autumn, a biographical documentary on Gordon Parks, was an unfinished project by the young director Craig Rice. Parks took control of it and overhauled it with a new script writer. I was brought in for additional photography to restructure and thread the gaps; interviews with Parks and him in the process of creating the book *Half Past Autumn* (a collection of photographs and essays in his later career) became a clear theme of the revision. There is a short segment when Parks is composing music for the film on the baby grand in his living room. Since he could not read or write music, he used his own system of notation with numerals and symbols, decipherable only by him. Sometimes he played on an electric keyboard, adding various instruments, mixing and

hiro narita. depth of field

> **HASKELL WEXLER** March 14, 2008
>
> Dear Hiro:
>
> I can't remember whether I wrote to compliment you for the Gordon Parks DVD.
>
> I just saw it again and want to be sure something you did in 1984 is appreciated.
>
> Regards,
> Haskell

Complimentary card on letterhead by cinematographer Haskell Wexler ASC

rerecording, all by himself. He told me that among all the media with which he engaged in his career he felt specially at ease with music. It just came to him, he said, finding its way through the cracks in his consciousness; an enigma in creativity.

In another part of the film, he painted an abstract landscape in water color and a few inches above it placed a sheet of clear glass. Then on the glass he placed a sea shell and photographed it looking straight down from few feet above, lit only by the desk lamps. The result was a beautiful, natural object floating against the opulent background. Parks did not have a studio, or fancy lights, but he created these poetic images in his living room surrounded by photos and manuscripts in various stages of editing.

With this film you received your third Primetime Emmy Awards nomination

When the film aired on television the original cinematographer Henry Adebonojo and I were nominated for Emmy, and Kodak

Hiro Narita with director Gordon Parks filming *Solomon Northup's Odyssey* (1984) in Savannah, Georgia

held a dinner party for the nominees of that year. Among the attendees were Vittorio Storaro, Haskell Wexler, and Stephen Goldblatt: acclaimed cinematographers I truly admired.

Prince Jack is a 1985 film directed by Bert Levitt which dramatizes some of the inner workings of the Kennedy administration. The movie covers the period from the Democratic National Convention in July 1960 to the autumn of 1963, just prior to the assassination of John F. Kennedy. What do you remember about the assassination of John Kennedy? You were a young student...

I heard a man shout out, "The president has been assassinated!" when I was working part time in an automobile supply shop as a student. In school the unthinkable news very much preoccupied us and it dominated our conversations in the cafeteria and the hallways; although I was not politically motivated, the shock wave knocked me off balance. And the Vietnam war escalation was more than just a rumor, a dark cloud hovering over our heads. Impending military draft haunted our age group and some schemed ways to avoid military service. Working on *Prince Jack,* twenty years after serving the Army, enlightened me about the entangled workings of covert political maneuvers beyond national concerns. It was a good education for me beyond my cinematographic one.

With The Blue Yonder *(1985) directed by Mark Rosman and produced by Walt Disney Television, you won The Cable ACE Award.*

Time traveling was a fascinating subject and this project was a genuinely enjoyable to work on. With Peter Cayote (*E.T. the Extra-Terrestrial*), Art Carney (*Jackie Gleason Show*), and Huckleberry Fox (*Terms of Endearment*) in the main cast, there were no elaborate sets or fancy contraptions. The child's imaginary world came alive on screen without visual effects. Can the boy go back to the past and change its events because he knew the outcome in the present? Director Rosman's idea to keep the past imaginary world real and accessible made this film honest and convincing. Since the costumes and the period cars and airplanes distinguished the past from the present, in lighting I kept the two worlds very similar, almost parallel with a small threshold between them, because the two time periods were experienced by the imaginative but innocent child. With such a small project I did not expect my work to be recognized by the industry, so the award was a pleasant surprise.

In the film the editorial consultant was Paul Hirsh, who cut a lot of the De Palma movies and won an Academy Award for Star Wars, *while the composer was David Shire, Academy Award winner for* Norma Rae. *What can you tell me about them?*

From the early 70s through the 90s was a very exciting and productive period in northern California, and I came across many editors. Pau Hirsh, Marsha Lucas, Richard Chew, and Walter Murch were among those I came to know. Later I met Paul Hirsh at an ILM reunion but I had forgotten he was the consultant editor on *The Blue Yonder*. I think he had a strong and creative input in the final cut. I did not meet David Shire since his involvement was in the post-production stage in Los Angeles.

In the cast there is Art Carney. He won the Academy Award for Best Actor for his 1974 performance as Harry Coombes, an elderly man going on the road with his pet cat, in Harry and Tonto (1974) *directed by Paul Mazursky. What do you remember about him?*

Veteran actor Art Carney was very pleasant and jovial on set and on top he had a good rapport with the young actor Fox. But at this time in his career, it was not easy for him to remember the whole dialogue and he often asked for cue-cards. We obliged him without hesitation.

Sylvester *is a 1985 family drama film directed by Tim Hunter and starring Richard Farnsworth and Melissa Gilbert; she, from 1974* to 1983, starred as Laura Ingalls Wilder on the NBC series Little House on the Prairie.

Richard Farnsworth (*Grey Fox, The Straight Story*) had an important presence in the film as a rancher and his lenient personality was a natural fixture in the story. He even drove his trailer and lived in it like a cowboy, avoiding hotels where he said he did not feel comfortable to stay. We filmed the large portion in Texas. For Gilbert, despite years on *Little House* series, this location must have been too gritty and uncomfortable, she had to endure a difficult adjustment. Then we moved to Kentucky for the dressage and equestrian competitions. This was a very different world in which the horses were treated and cared like royalty in luxurious stables; a very expensive sport, if you can call it such. *Silvester*, for its relatively simple plot and story, was not an easy project for me. I tried to figure out why. Was it my unfamiliarity with the subject or the locations? I can only surmise that I was not challenging myself wholeheartedly in the project because my energy in considerable part was taken up by managing the crew. For instance, for the first time in my career, I had to dismiss a person due to his drinking problem on set, a major concern for safety and maintaining solidarity among us. At one point I had to replace a camera operator who had a stroke while filming a scene! Being a director of photography required hidden responsibilities for overseeing the crew's harmony and keeping the production fluid.

You also worked briefly on Blue Velvet *(1986) a noir mystery thriller film written and directed by David Lynch. The film stars Kyle MacLachlan, Isabella Rossellini, Dennis Hopper and Laura Dern. The title of the film is taken from the homonymous song by Bobby Vinton, sung in the film by Isabella Rossellini in a nightclub. What sequence did you shoot and where?*

Without much briefing, I arrived in North Carolina to do some pick-ups for *Blue Velvet*. The studio was called De Laurentiis

Studios in those days. David Lynch, whom I had met at social gatherings in northern California, showed me a large ear he had sculpted himself and told me he needed a slow tracking shot into the earhole. Then he needed close-ups of cockroaches crawling in the grass, seen from ground level with the camera stealthy tracking forward. We used a snorkel lens system to achieve this. To slow down the insects' rapid movements the handler may have sprayed a blast of dry ice cloud over the cockroaches before each take. This was an unusual experience, to say the least. And finally, I had to shoot an establishing exterior shot of a town. Lynch suggested I consult with the first unit cinematographer Fred Elmes, because he used some special filter. Elmes explained to me over the phone that with the mid focal length lenses he used a behind-the-lens black net and shot at F5.6-stops or wider aperture (requiring neutral density filters in front of the lens when the normal exposure is above F5.6). These specific requirements, I believed, added to the unique look of the film.

What do you remember of David Lynch, considered one of the most brilliant and visionary American directors? He is also a painter and visual artist, in addition to Blue Velvet *he has directed works such as* The Elephant Man, Dune, Wild at Heart, Mulholland Drive *and the tv-series* Twin Peaks.

In the short time I spent with Lynch, he was unassuming and soft-spoken. He enjoyed, as I watched him, tinkering with the big ear as with a piece of sculpture and kept touching it up with paint until we were ready to roll the camera. Come to think of it, there are several paintings in *Blue Velvet* that are known to be Lynch's own work.

Fire with Fire *is a 1986 American romantic drama film directed by Duncan Gibbins about a young woman from a Catholic boarding school who runs away with an escapee from a nearby prison camp. The film stars Virginia Madsen, Craig Sheffer, Jon Polito.*

hiro narita. depth of field

The film was shot and produced under the original title Captive Hearts, *but was changed to* Fire with Fire *just prior to the movie's theater release, is that correct?*

That is correct. The actual title change came after we finished the production. Director Gibbins mentioned briefly that he wanted an edge to the title; he wanted the film to imply more than just a romantic story. I also think there was another film in production by the same title, *Captive Hearts*, with Pat Morita in it.

What is your memory of the protagonist Virginia Madsen? A few years earlier she had played the role of Princess Irulan in Dune *(1984) directed by David Lynch.*

I went to Gibbins' office to get a new copy of the script and he simply said, this is Virginia Madsen. She looked familiar but I did not know her name, nor could I place her in a movie immediately. As I was leaving the office, it occurred to me I had seen her in *Dune*, and I whispered to Gibbins, is she the actress in *Dune*? He nodded with a smile. Madsen was cast to play the lead, Lisa. In my recollection she was very reserved among a dozen of vocal and animated young actors whom Gibbins dealt enthusiastically, enjoying every moment of the interactions.

Duncan Gibbins was a British film and music video director (Glenn Frey, Eurythmics, Wham!): Fire with Fire *was his first feature film. He died in the massive wildfires that plagued the Southern California region in 1993, he was forty-one years old. What memory do you have of him?*

I received a call from Gibbins' girlfriend when I was working in Los Angeles, informing me of his critical condition in hospital. I learned that he escaped from his burning house but returned to it to save his cat. I rushed to the hospital but was not allowed to visit him due to his dire condition. A few days after Gibbins passed away; it was a big shock to me, needless to say. I cherish his tireless energy and humor while working on *Fire with Fire*; what an ironic title it turned out to be!

Amerika is a television miniseries that was broadcast in 1987 on ABC directed by Donald Wrye. The miniseries inspired a novelization entitled Amerika: The Triumph of the American Spirit. *Amerika starred Kris Kristofferson, Mariel Hemingway, Sam Neill, Robert Ulrich, Lara Flynn Boyle. A TV miniseries that predicted a Russian takeover of America?*

Years earlier, I filmed a documentary Donald Wrye produced for the US Information Agency about the life of a married couple who owned a semi-truck and hitched cargo-trailers for hire and drove long distances across the States. He was familiar with my documentary work as well as my recent narrative films.

Amerika was a monumental miniseries consisting of seven episodes (each approximately 1 ½ hours long and the script nearly 600 pages long) that spanned seven months of production. Photographically, it presented me with two distinct visual palettes: the bleak winter farmland, the spawning ground of the resistance against the foreign invader (filmed in Nebraska) and the world of political power maneuvers (filmed in Toronto, Canada).

Wrye described to me *Amerika:* although the fictional story is set in the future, it called for a docudrama approach, the sense of immediacy, the now and the here. Against the anarchic setting many scenes dealt with armed conflict; tanks and helicopters clearing squatters out of their shacks. This was my first introduction to a quantity of pyrotechnics and armed vehicles, and, I cannot over emphasize that safety was the utmost concern for the actors, the large number of extras, as well as for the crew. Many stunt men and women in costumes were spread out among the extras, to ensure their safety. We received thorough briefings with diagrams with each set-up, and we rehearsed to avoid mishaps and accident (we nearly had a serious one). Today, I assume many of the dangerous images would be digitally created and physical dangers avoided.

hiro narita. depth of field

What can you tell me about the locations and your photographic work?

Built in studios in Toronto were the ¾ scale sets of the House Chamber and a section of the US Capitol Rotunda, some of the largest I had ever dealt with. Fortunately for me, the experienced Canadian lighting crew was very helpful, setting and rigging a multiplicity of lights. I would explain to them in terms of light and shadow, foot-candle when needed to be more specific, and let them translate what I said into exact configurations of lights to achieve the look I was after. Come to think of it, this approach had been my working method with most lighting crews wherever I worked, relying on their expertise, but was rather broad and technically unspecific on my part. On this project I used Agfa film stock with tabular crystal grains (simply called T grain) which reduced the scattering of light, producing sharper images compared to the films on the market at the time. Although T grain was already in use in Kodak still negatives, Agfa was the first to apply it in motion picture stock.

The director Wyre during his career has been nominated for an Oscar twice in the category of Best Documentary, Short Subjects for An Impression of John Steinbeck: Writer *(1969) and for* The Numbers Begin With the River *(1971). He directed the series with a lot of dedication and attention, given the length of the project.*

In his earlier career Wrye had written, produced, and directed many distinguished documentary films and his organizational skill was extraordinary. *Amerika* was no exception. Wrye's responsibility extended beyond the actors' performance and structural cohesion, but, as the writer of the series, he continued revising and improving the script late into the evening. During the lengthy production a distinguished ensemble of actors took part in the mini-series, sometimes working out of continuity in two countries. To keep the story's continuity in check, I paid much

indies to studios

attention to visual flow, and sometimes to the contrast, to emphasized the two worlds, poles apart.

No Man's Land is a 1987 American crime film written by Dick Wolf directed by Peter Werner, and stars Charlie Sheen, D. B. Sweeney, and Randy Quaid.

A large segment of this crime drama, both interiors and exteriors, was shot at night on locations. Making use of available lights, street lights and building lights, for instance, I had to maintain the exposure balance with our movie lights. I often resorted to near wide-open apertures on the lenses, resulting in a shallow depth of field. A risky attempt, but the images had a certain quality befitting the story. The project was produced by Imagine Entertainment, co-chaired by Ron Howard (*American Graffiti*), and because of this project–with the US labor law on my side–I was finally accepted on the Hollywood industry roster. A friendship or a brief working relationship precipitate you unexpectedly on a new path in your career, and this project launched me into the Hollywood film industry.

When you first worked on No Man's Land *with Charlie Sheen, did you tell him about your first meeting with his father Martin for Apocalypse now?*

I mentioned to Sheen about filming his father and seeing him as a young boy. He remembered visiting the Coppola estate, but not so much about the filming itself.

"I only steal Porsche," says the character portrayed by Charlie Sheen, the millionaire playboy Ted Varrick suspected of car thefts and the murder of a detective. In the film there are a lot of action scenes related to cars. Was it complicated to shoot them?

There were many action scenes involving car chases, crashes, even a semi-truck being hit. Second unit director and stunt co-

ordinator Jim Arnett (*The Rocketeer*) and his stunt crew meticulously prepared and rehearsed before the camera crew arrived. From his experience Arnett suggested the best camera angles for certain shots. In that sense the shooting was not complicated for me. I simply had to make sure the camera operators did not miss the actions. One chase sequence in a warehouse was assigned to the second unit (Roy Wagner, ASC), since it was too elaborate and time-consuming for the main unit to carry out.
With many driving scenes involving Sheen and D. B. Sweeney we had one car always rigged with a camera mount and set aside its double for the drive-by in order to save production time. Any moving vehicle, even those not involved in stunt actions, had to be driven by professionals to choreograph the precise timing of the actions.

Peter Werner is essentially a television director, among other things winner of an Oscar for best short film with In the Region of Ice *(1971). How was your collaboration?*

No Mans's Land might have been Peter Werner's first feature film, but coming from a documentary background he had a strong sense of spontaneity and addressed the project with an open and keen mind. We had a very good rapport and I enjoyed the project in spite of the story that dealt with a lot of car chases and shootings, an unfamiliar territory for me at the time.

In the film in a small role (that of a waiter) appears Brad Pitt, his first appearance on the big screen. Do you have any memory of this?

I read that Pitt's earliest film appearance was in *No Man's Land* as a waiter, and I had to check it myself on DVD. In several nightclub and café scenes in the film, I could not find him nor remember him being in the film. He must have looked very different then. This brings back a memory of Naomi Judd–the famous country singer and mother of Ashley and Wynonna Judd–who

indies to studios

was a production assistant on *More American Graffiti*. She even appeared in a dancing scene as an extra. Nobody imagined her as a future five-time Grammy Award winner and the Country Music Hall of Fame inductee. She was a very conscientious, energetic worker and she would give away her promo cassette recordings of songs recorded at her home–I received one, but sadly, I don't know what I did with it. Another moment in my life crossing with someone destined to reach greatness.

The Unbearable Lightness of Being is a 1988 drama film, an adaptation of the 1984 novel of the same name by Milan Kundera, directed by Philip Kaufman and starring Daniel Day-Lewis, Juliette Binoche and Lena Olin. What can you tell me about your collaboration on this film?

After the main unit in Europe had completed, Kaufman needed a few additional scenes in a northern California house with Sabina (Lena Olin). Although I was familiar with Nykvist's work, I had to study his mastery of light, his subtle use of ambience and mood

Hiro Narita (back to camera), director Philip Kaufman and Barbara Parker Narita. Photo by Pamela Gentile

he created in many of his movies. It might have taken me more than a lifetime to understand and learn it, but I tried to emulate his work in shorthand, at least I tried to make my work integrate into the tonality of his work in this film. Kaufman gave me an anecdotal account of Nykvist's work: simple but imaginative.

What can you tell me about Kaufman, with whom you previously worked on The Right Stuff *(1983)?*

I was also fascinated by Kaufman's directing on this US segment. As if writing a draft about Olin's character or sketching her on a piece of drawing paper, he studied the space and the light before settling on the actor's blocking and the camera angles, some of which seemed extemporaneous and incidental. Through a window Sabina sees a mailman approaching the house, when she interrupts her painting overcome with an ominous sensation and anticipation. Cut to her reading the letter on a beach stroked by the setting sun. Very simple and lyrical. But in the final film, I realized that the rhythm of the scene was in concert with what came before and after this scene. Some shots never made it into the film, yet I appreciated that fragments can articulate more than the whole when seen in context. The film was edited by Walter Murch, a long-time collaborator of Francis Coppola.

Have you met Sven Nykvist FSF-ASC, Ingmar Bergman's legendary collaborator and winner of two Academy Awards?

I wish I had an opportunity to meet him, but the chance never materialized. Perhaps he was already engaged in another project in Europe. I embraced his work on *Persona* and *Fanny and Alexander*, among others, have left profound impressions on me.

Speaking of the great Swedish director, widely considered one of the most accomplished and influential filmmakers of all time, what about him? Were you fascinated by his authorial poetics? He addressed the human condition with his films, like few others ...

From the 60s on as European films started to fill art houses, Bergman's films stood out, attracting young audiences with existential questions on morality, loneliness, alienation, introspective issues that my generation were curious about but did not dwell on. His films somehow made it okay to talk about them in the open. The exotic Swedish ambience was made accessible to us through Nykvist's striking cinematography. I was too young and naïve to understand Bergman's tortured characters, but still, embraced in stark and shimmering images, I could sense the power of implication. As I grew older, Bergman's recurring questions became more transparent.

With producer and director Frank Marshall (with Kathleen Kennedy and Steven Spielberg, he was one of the founders of Amblin Entertainment) you worked on two short-film (live-action segments): Tummy Trouble *(1989) and* Roller Coaster Rabbit *(1990). They are the first two animated short films (with mixed media ending) produced following the success of the film* Who framed Roger Rabbit *(1988) directed by Robert Zemeckis. What do you think of this animation technique?*

Robert Zemeckis' live-action-animation combination totally revolutionized this not-so-new technique by introducing complex camera movements–I heard Disney was initially against it because it opened up many difficulties in animation. Thanks to Zemeckis' conviction, the tradition was broken. As I understand, the live action footage was printed and enlarged frame by frame, and by tracing each frame, the animators drew the characters, assimilating their intricate actions with camera movements. The visual effects supervisor Ken Ralston and his crew at ILM then added 3-dimensional quality by creating realistic shadows and smoothing out the animated characters' actions. Filming these short live-action movies showed how daunting it must have been to shoot the original film. For our short film we did not have stuffed animated characters on the set; instead, we had blue targets all over representing the character's movements, and director Marshall had to coordinate precisely the timing of the actors acting against the imaginary characters. In a sense this live-action/animation technique tilled the ground for the future live/digital combination technique.

You collaborated with director Joe Johnston in his first two films: Honey, I Shrunk the Kids *(1989) and* The Rocketeer *(1991).* Honey, I Shrunk the Kids *is a 1989 American comic science fiction film that was one of the most successful sci-fi comedies of the cinema's history. It was the directorial debut of Joe Johnston, while Rick Moranis stars as Wayne Szalinski, the inventor who accidentally shrinks his children.*

I was in Mexico City, already preparing the film with director Stewart Gordon (*Re-Animator*). Unfortunately, he became ill and his doctor ordered him to return home. Producer Tom Smith (*The Arrival*), a former ILM manager I worked with in the past, recruited Johnston immediately to resume production. A brilliant choice. Having worked at ILM for many years as a story sequence creator on the *Star Wars* series, Johnston had extensive experi-

Hiro Narita filming *Honey, I Shrunk the Kids* (Disney Pictures)

Honey, I Shrunk the Kids (1989) directed
by Joe Johnston sitting on the rock

Honey, I Shrunk the Kids (1989) directed
by Joe Johnston behind the ant

ence in compositing live action with miniature robotic creatures, and a host of visual effects. On *Honey, I Shrunk the Kids*, he now had to deal with over-scale sets.

When Johnston joined the project many changes were introduced in the script, I believe, by Johnston and additional writers, but much of the over-size grass set was already built at Churubusco Studios based on the original script. The main house and the neighborhood (both interior and exterior) were designed with Johnston's recommendation based on the research we did together with the production designer in my home town, Petaluma; the town embodying a generic Americana, a blend of neo-Victorian homes, was a perfect choice. My gaffer Steve Mathis (*The Rocketeer, The Time Machine*), with whom I had developed a working relationship since *No Man's Land*, was resourceful, along with the Mexican members of the crew. Communicating in broken Spanish, they hung skylights and placed large units between the blades of grass. Since Churubusco was not equipped for the enormous scale of the sets, many of the big lights, especially 10 Ks and HMIs along with many accessories, were brought in from California. As for the camera equipment, a branch of Panavision Cameras was conveniently located in the city and they supplied the equipment, responding promptly to our additional needs.

The film was also inspired by The Incredible Shrinking Man *(1957) directed by Jack Arnold. Did you see Arnold's movie before filming?*

No, I did not see the film, although I was aware of it.

What do you remember of the actor Moranis, back from successful films like Little Shop of Horrors *(1986) directed by Frank Oz?*

Rick Moranis and Matt Frewer (*Max Headroom*) were perpetually amusing and witty, keeping us entertained as if watching a comedy sketch every day. Moranis, in spite of his stardom, was down to earth, regular, and very cooperative with our technical demands; in some scenes he performed his own stunts avidly. Frewer also was a big hit in a comedy television series, but, like Moranis, he was convivial and regular. Both being Canadian I am sure they enjoyed each other's company. With Frewer in 1994, I filmed *Long Shadows*, a PBS American Masters series in which he played scholar Edwin O. Reischauer, the US Ambassador to Japan during the Kennedy Administration. I found him a very different persona, not a trace of the comedic character I knew before. And we traveled to Japan to film segments of the story.

How was the set made? How did you photograph the environments in which the miniature actors move with respect to the objects?

Initially, the blades of grass (some nearly 25 feet heigh) made of styrofoam and covered in fiber glass skin were very heavy, and each one had to be propped up by wires from the ceiling. I suggested the special effects crew should attach additional wires to the blades so they can shake them a little, as if they were swaying in the breeze, to give life to otherwise static blades. When you look at a blade of grass through a microscope, it is entirely covered in translucent hair-like spikes; amazing attributes of nature. Replicating a live specimen, the blades close to the camera were copiously covered with plastic needles, and sprayed with diluted glycerin to look damp.
Imagining what it would be like in the forest of grass where dapples of sunlight penetrated, I wanted to create a spooky, unfamiliar world from a child's perspective. But Disney were not too enthusiastic when the early dailies were screened, and I had to tone down my initial approach, giving away the emotional realism over the movie fantasy. Disney might have remembered my earlier work on *Never Cry Wolf*, and worried that the fantasy/comedy for the young audience may end up being too serious. As the filming progressed, settling into a routine, I received a new comment from Disney saying, contrary to their earlier remarks, I should take dramatic license and not be hesitant about shadowy areas. The change in their tone surprised me but I was happy to

hiro narita. depth of field

hear it. I believe, equally true in any cinematic storytelling, once you establish the setting early on, you need not show everything all the time. Let the viewer fill in the unseen part in his mind.
The large mechanized ant was created by ILM, operated by several puppeteers on the set. The giant scorpion, on the other hand, was a stop-motion animation created by Phil Tippett (*Jurassic Park*) in California and composited into live actions. Countless visual effects, special effects and blue screen shots–a special unit working simultaneously in another studio near us–were woven together to make this fanciful movie come alive.

By the way, Tummy Trouble *had its theater release in June 23, 1989 with* Honey, I Shrunk the Kids, *do you remember this anecdote?*

No, I did not know it.

Hollywood

1990s-2000s

The Rocketeer *(1991) that stars Bill Campbell, Jennifer Connelly is based upon the character of the same name created by comic book artist and writer Dave Stevens. Set in 1938 Los Angeles* The Rocketeer *tells the story of stunt pilot Cliff Secord who stumbles upon a hidden rocket-powered jet pack that he thereafter uses to fly without the need of an aircraft.*

Johnston did not want a comic book-to-movie transplant with *The Rocketeer*; rather, he wanted to treat it like any other narrative story, a period drama but with a fantasy element imbedded in this case. The story takes place around the mid-1930s in Los Angeles, and during my research I realized that color movies were rare then, they were in their infancy. I drew instead my inspiration from the color palette of movie posters from that period. Did they express the idealism, the post-art deco influence of the time? I am not so sure. The set and the costume design definitely added a visual flavor to the film.

What did the director ask you about the photographic look of the film?

Johnston asked me specifically how we can capture the unpolluted blue sky of the 30s in California. It was a big conundrum. After some pondering, I tested a color-enhancer filter for outdoor. The filter intensified the red and blue layers of the film emulsion and the result increased the blue of the sky, but people's

hiro narita. depth of field

skin turned unnaturally warm at the same time. After consulting with a Technical Lab colorist, we settled on a set of timing lights that kept the sky bluer than it was–of course we had to avoid blue costumes that would get intensified–and reduced the overall warm color. In another words, we reduced the effect of the color enhancement in the red layer of the emulsion to an acceptable range, in my view. I think I found the solution that kept abreast with the flavor of the period. The project did not utilize computer graphics or digital color grading–long before their time; it was produced in the traditional way, incorporating miniature, blue screen, traveling backdrops, and optical compositing. We even built large ¾ scale sections of the airship that were combined with the miniatures.

How did you prepare for the filming? Did you have any reference points from films of the past?

During the pre-production I thought of Fellini's *8 ½* I had seen many years ago. There was something outside logic and linear storytelling that felt very real in the film. Until I saw the film few times, I did not realize there were light changes in the middle of scenes that were more than eye-catching lighting ef-

Hiro Narita filming *The Rocketeer* (1991)

fects; they gave life to the sensations and emotional rhythms. Even though *8 ½* was in black and white, I thought the dance sequence in the South Sea Club was a great moment to explore that concept. The prerecorded music was repeatable precisely with the big band pantomiming it. So, my electronic dimmer-board operator and I programed subtle light changes synchronized with the music. I think they heightened the moments like modulating musical notes, breathing life into the scene, without making obvious statements. I like images that are emotionally right even if they are not rational or astute. Discovering what light does, what people see in it and feel from it, visual experiences that you can't pinpoint yet touch your heart, is very important to me.

The visual effects were designed and created by George Lucas' Industrial Light & Magic (ILM), exact?

Ken Ralston (*Back to the Future, Forrest Gump*) at ILM was in charge of the visual effects and he created exciting images with miniatures and ingenious compositing. The large airship hovering over the Griffith Observatory building and Hollywood at night, and eventually exploding in the air was one such example; ILM's extraordinary skill and Johnston's exciting story telling were on full display.

It is true you used Agfa on The Rocketeer, *just for the South Seas Club sequence? Why?*

Production designer Jim Bissell (*E.T., 300*) chose a dark green for the walls in the South Sea Club (two-story set built in the largest Disney studio), an elegant signature color of the period night club. From my experience dealing with the color green, I was concerned that it may shift toward blue or darker green than it looked to our eyes. The initial test, as I suspected, showed the walls bluer than Bissell envisioned. I added light green jell to the lights around the walls to enhance the color but it effected the

Cover of the magazine American Cinematographer dedicated to the film *The Rocketeer* (June, 1991). Courtesy of American Cinematographer

hollywood

The Rocketeer's frame: South Sea Club sequence

actors nearby. I proposed testing it with Agfa film I was familiar with from shooting *Amerika*. Knowing Disney was contractually obligated to use only Kodak stock processed by Technicolor Lab, I went ahead anyway. The result was satisfactory to Bissell and we showed both Kodak and Agfa tests to the studio executives asking them to choose without telling them one was shot in Agfa. They chose Agfa and allowed us to use it only for the South Sea Club scenes. At the time, Agfa film incorporated T grain in the emulsion, making the image sharper, and its green emulsion reproduced a truer hue than Kodak stock. Interestingly, some cinematographers shot Kodak and printed on Agfa or Fuji, or shot on Fuji and printed on Kodak, making the best use of their characteristics. Gradually, they all became similar to one another, eventually adding a cyan layer to the emulsion to counteract the effect of florescent and industrial lights.

Jennifer Connely debuted in cinema very young, playing a girl (young Deborah) to dance in the gangster epic Once Upon a Time in America *(1984) directed by Sergio Leone. Although having little screen time, the few minutes she was on-screen were enough to reveal her talent. Had you seen the Leone movie, photographed by Tonino Delli Colli AIC?*

Tonino Delli Colli's work was excellent, I remember it well and I recognized his versatile talent in *Life is Beautiful*.

So, what do you remember of Connely?

Jennifer Connely was one potential Jenny among the young actresses director Johnston and I screen tested for *The Rocketeer*. I saw her in *Labyrinth* and *Career Opportunity* (photographed by Don McAlpine), but she was in very different roles. But when she appeared in the 30s dress and make-up for the test, she simply stood out from all others, and standing next to Bill Campbell (*Rocketeer*) Connely became the most convincing Jenny.

Leone was famous before Once Upon a Time in America, *for reinventing the western genre. Do you like westerns by the way?*

My favorite western is *High Noon*. What we call "western" deals with a wide range of stories that embrace a hero, his conflict, and finally his triumph, in a nutshell; stories are suspenseful but easy to follow. They do not have to take place in the wild west either. I think the popularity lies in the universality of the basic concept. Spaghetti western and Asian western are all closely associated with those of America. But the ones by Leone were stylish, irresistable, and very entertaining.

In 1989, you photographed the visual effects in the Steven Spielberg movie Always. *The film is a remake of the 1943 romantic drama* A Guy Named Joe *directed by Victor Fleming and set during World War II. What can you tell me about?*

Helmed by Joe Johnston, I photographed a large miniature airplane (around 14 feet in wing span) flying through miniature forest fires at night, as well as day. My main objective was to achieve a seamless match with the first unit shots in spite of differences of scale and often limited availability of the first unit footage to compare.

While testing exposure and color-film in a large former steel factory–I noticed that the fire by itself lacked drama in my eyes, and in the film. It needed some help to make it look real on screen as I pictured it in my head. I consulted with the lighting supervisor at ILM, and he suggested hanging Maxi Brutes with orange filter from the ceiling along the plane's path, each lamp connected to a flicker box. I then proposed placing a dozen of par lights on the floor randomly, face-up to the plane, also connected to flicker boxes. They convincingly added flaring effect to the airplane, and when it flew through, the fire looked ablaze. The burning trees were Christmas trees, some attached to vertical propane flame bars. During the course of filming the plane, I was told over 1200 trees were set ablaze. To compensate the scale of the miniature to that of the real, the camera ran at 40 frames instead of the usual 24 frames, slowing down the flare motion. Encountering these unusual special effects gave me much insight into the art of cinematography.

In the cast of Always *there were Richard Dreyfuss, Holly Hunter, John Goodman, Audrey Hepburn, who was on her latest film. Did you get to know any of them?*

My involvement was mainly with the miniature airplane. I filmed one green screen shot at ILM with Richard Dreyfuss ascending the stairs to heaven, the finale of the movie with Spielberg directing.

What do you remember about your cinematography for Star Trek VI: The Undiscovered Country *(1991)? It is the sixth feature film based on the Star Trek series (created by Gene Roddenberry) and the last with the full original cast. Nicholas Meyer was directing a chapter of the saga for the second time, after directing* Star Trek II: The Wrath of Khan *(1982).*

hiro narita. depth of field

Director Nicholas Meyer and producer Steven-Charles Jaffe visited me on the set of *The Rocketeer* at Disney Studios when I was filming a scene in the South Sea Club set. They were fascinated by the computer-guided lighting system, which I explained them expedited day-to-day filming. Meyer felt comfortable with my working method and I was brought onboard *Star Trek VI; Undiscovered Country*. I told him upfront that I was not a Trekkie, nor did I know much about *Star Trek*. He responded he was happy that I was not. He did not want preconceived ideas set in motion or becoming the launching pad for his upcoming movie.

How did you deal with such a famous film saga? How did you set up your photography?

A challenge I faced was that there was a tradition in *Star Trek* history: the sets and, to a certain degree, in the visual, because

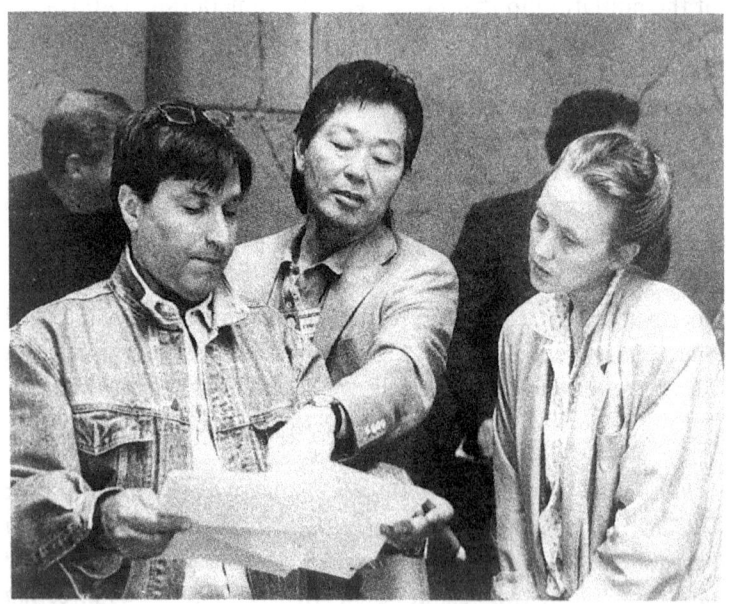

Star Trek VI: The Undiscovered Country. Director Nicholas Meyer, Hiro Narita and camera operator Kristin Glover. Courtesy of American Cinematographer

A storyboard from *Star Trek VI* (Zero gravity scene)

Cover of the magazine American Cinematographer dedicated to the film *Star Trek VI* (January, 1992). Courtesy of American Cinematographer

of its success. And to reduce production cost we had to recycle some old sets with minor redecorating. Meyer wanted to evolve and update images from the previous Star Treks, including the ones he wrote or directed. He wanted the interior of the Starship Enterprise to look older and used with updated instrument panels, since it was mothballed for years and reactivated for the story. But we met with some resistance from those attached to the previous franchise, and looking back, there were compromises in the production beyond the director's control.

What was the contribution of the ILM? What can you tell me about the special effects?

A new computer graphics software, developed by ILM for *Abyss*, was put to use to create the purple blood droplets floating in zero-gravity space. And the morphing program helped shape-shift Martia (Iman) into other characters. ILM also provided Starship Enterprise and other spaceships in action captured by the motion-control camera using miniatures. As for the main unit filming, Meyer wanted to rely on on-the-set, in-the-camera effects practiced by the industry in the past. One example: a Klingon was blasted away in a shooting battle in a passageway, and the impact flings him backwards. We turned the corridor 90 degrees in the vertical position and as the Klingon was shot, he was quickly pulled up by the wire cables away from the camera pointing up. When the footage is projected, the image returning to the horizontal perspective, the Klingon looked as if his body is floating away in the impact. Using practical tools and sets, the illusions created were remarkable; homage to the tradition of Hollywood magic. Digital technology now enables the creation of images with layers of visual components without sacrificing image quality, and significantly, it frees the production from building complicated, often unattainable physical sets. With *Star Trek VI* we were finally reaching the end of traditional movie making. Just a few years later, Spielberg's *Jurassic Park* revolutionized it forever with unprecedented digital graphics and effects.

hiro narita. depth of field

In this movie you worked with a different crew because the people you normally worked with were unavailable. You hired one of the few female camera operators, Kristen Glover, who occasionally manned the B camera on The Rocketeer.

My regular gaffer was not available on this film and I asked Ramon Rao, an assistant gaffer on my previous films, to be the chief lighting gaffer. He showed aesthetic taste and, of course, ample technical expertise for the role.
Kristin Glover became "A" camera operator for the film. In the early 90s the Cinematographer Guild was still a closely guarded, if not male-dominated, guild. I first worked with Kristen Glover when she was working as assistant cameraperson with Stephen H. Burum on *The Bee Gees Special*. Besides being an assistant, she was a committed advocate of diversity and equity in the guild membership, which I too strongly agreed with and believed in. By the time *The Rocketeer* came along she had advanced to camera operating and I hired her as B camera operator for the dance scene in the South Sea Club. I recognized her talent and asked her to be "A" camera operator on *Star Trek VI*, and subsequently on *Hocus Pocus*. I am happy to see that in recent years many female cinematographers are making significant contributions to the art of cinematography. I felt recognition of their artistry in the industry was overdue.

Because of the tight schedule and the relatively large size of the courtroom set, did you use a timesaving technique you'd employed for The Rocketeer's *South Seas Club sequence, with electronic dimmers?*

The computer-assisted lighting system was gaining popularity (I believe Storaro used it in *Dick Tracy*). Although it was complex and time-consuming to prepare, once the shooting began the system greatly reduced the down time between camera set-ups. It also made complicated lighting cues precisely repeatable, and subtle adjustments of the luminance was easily and quickly con-

hollywood

trolled from the floor. The only time I sent a crew up onto the cat walks was to physically reposition lights. By reducing the lighting adjustment time for new camera angles, I believed the actors in turn maintained their concentration on their performance.

In the court room scene located deep underground, the main source of light was a narrow bright shaft cast from an opening of the vertical tunnel above, and the ambient light came from a few space lights and from the long staff-torches held by the Klingons in attendance. I wanted to hang a strong spotlight from above, aiming straight down to the center of the courtroom arena where Captain Kirk (William Shatner) and Dr. McCoy (De Forest Kelley) are interrogated by Chan (Christopher Plumer). Rao suggested instead, for safety's sake, we hang a plexiglass mirror in the center of the ceiling at 45 degrees and place a xenon spotlight outside the set aimed at the mirror. The shaft of light deflected straight down to the floor, avoiding any potential accident above the actors' heads or overheating of the light cast down. It was a very prudent solution. I over-exposed the shaft of light by at least F2 stops, emphasizing the dark oppressive court room and the difficulty the characters were having to see the court room audience.

William Shatner and Leonard Nimoy are best known for their portrayal of Captain James T. Kirk and Spock of the USS Enterprise in the Star Trek *franchise. What can you tell me about them?*

Both Shatner and Nimoy had been with the Star Trek series since its inception in the television series, and they had both directed the movie previously. So, their input in *The Undiscovered Country* was consequential. Shatner's enthusiasm sometimes overstepped and he suggested where the camera should be for his close-ups, but Myer was very much in control, I might add, with a good sense of humor. Nimoy on the other hand was deeply steeped in the story–he is credited as one of the concept writers–not simply as Spock but as a story consultant.

At one point during the production, Nimoy was also involved

in a stage performance of *Love Letters,* a two-person play, in a small local theater one weekend. I went to see it out of curiosity and I was awe-struck by his nuanced performance–shedding the make-up and the iconic character Spock at Paramount Studios–he displayed his compelling talent on the stage. I mentioned my reaction to Nimoy's stage performance back on the *Star Trek* set, and he was very happy to hear that I saw him only as the character immersed in the play.

For this movie, you proposed Agfa film to Paramount, but they refused and then you used Kodak?

With the successful result of Agfa film in *Amerika*–over a million feet was exposed–and *The Rocketeer,* however partial its use, I recommended Paramount Pictures to use it for the upcoming Star Trek. Predictably, some studios in Hollywood maintained tight relationships with Kodak, and Paramount was one of them I could not persuade.

Gene Roddenberry died within 48 hours of viewing this film. It was later dedicated to his memory. Have you ever met him?

Along with the member of the cast, I was invited to a lunch held by Nimoy and his wife in their backyard to celebrate the kick-off before the filming commenced. Nick Meyer introduced me to Gene Roddenberry who was in his wheel chair and in poor health. It was a brief, courtesy greeting.

You mentioned earlier that you also worked on The Bee Gees Special *(1979) directed by Louis J. Horvitz. You collaborated as an additional camera operator...*

This particular shoot is very fragmented in my memory. What remains distinctly in my experience is that my camera was positioned very close to a stack of giant speakers and I was having a chest pain while filming. A sound mixer told me at the end of the

hollywood

first day that the loud decibel and the powerful vibration from the speakers were disrupting my heart beat, and he suggested I cover my chest with sound damping material. In addition, he warned that extremely loud music could have an adverse effect on my sense of balance! After the first day of the shoot, a gaffer gave me a small thin sheet of lead used in the power generator for noise reduction. The second day of the shoot was without an audience and I taped the lead sheet around my chest and wore it like a vest. I felt much better. Because of this unexpected incident and distraction, my memory of the concert is very muddled, most has slipped away.

You worked in the TV movie Plymouth *(1991). It tells the story of the residents of a town displaced by an industrial accident agree to take over a failing mining base on the Moon as their new place to live and work. It was directed by Lee David Zlotoff better known as the creator of the TV series* MacGyver. *What about the movie?*

The project was originally set to be a pilot for a TV series but it ended up as a one-time TV movie. We had enormous sets built to last for the series–interiors and exteriors of the moon–but our effort was short-lived. Cindy Picket from *Amerika* was cast in the lead role and we reminisced about its long arduous filming.

With the director Lucille Carra you worked on two documentaries The Inland Sea *(1991) and* Dvořák and America *(2000). The first is based on the travel memoir by Donald Richie. Twenty years earlier in 1991 Richie had published his book – a travel classic – titled* The Inland Sea; *Richie wrote about the Japanese people, the culture of Japan, and especially Japanese cinema, including his volume on Akira Kurosawa. Also wrote the English subtitles for Akira Kurosawa's films* Throne of Blood *(1957),* Red Beard *(1965),* Kagemusha *(1980) and* Dreams *(1990). The documentary was narrated by Richie himself. What did working in Japan mean for you?*

When Lucille Carra approached me about working on *The Inland Sea*, I was very excited because it was based on Donald

hiro narita. depth of field

Richie's travel-journal published in 1971. Richie's observation of Japanese culture and its people are insightful, intimate, and his wealth of knowledge on Japanese cinema is exceptional. Carra said to me that though I had once lived in Japan, having been away long enough, I could now see it with a new perspective. She, an American and I, an expatriate, could cast light on Richie's experience in Japan filtered through his prose, his mastery of storytelling. She was clear that the film was not a literal visualization of Richie's journal, because time has passed and so much of Japan, at least on the surface, had changed since his travel; it is, she said, an observation of and experience in Japan by a foreigner, an outsider. There is an advantage in being an outsider, Richie once said; his mistakes are forgiven and his perception of Japan not restrained by any commonly perceived or ethnocentric notion. I felt many of his assumptions ring true; I was not quite an outsider but not a genuine insider any longer. It is interesting

The Inland Sea (1991): far left (background) producer Brian Cotnoir, left director/producer Lucille Carra, Hiro Narita (center), right Ellen Wood assistant camera, far right (background) Larry Richards translator in Sanagimijima island in the Inland Sea of Japan

21 iii 91

Dear Hiro:

Just back from Shikoku. Went to Takamatsu again, and again to Ritsurin Koen . . . _in the snow_. The weather since the day you left has been like that: rain, fog, sleet, and now snow. So you and the crew really hit the weather window. And then this morning Lucille called with news of the first cut and how absolutely delighted she is with it. She says the footage looks terrific, and that it cuts like a dream since you edited in camera for them and everything fits. And so I am taking this opportunity now to do what I had intended doing earlier which is to write and tell you how pleased and happy and proud I am that you shot the film of my book. You were my first choice and I could not be more pleased that you agreed to create this for us. I will be getting a tape first week of next month. So will Takemitsu. And so will probably you. Can hardly wait.

And, many, many thanks for making this film.

My very best to you and to Barbara.

Yours,

Donald Richie

Letter of thanks for Narita's work on *The Inland Sea*, written by book author Donald Richie

to hear Richie say, in addition, that his first-person singular voice is a persona, quite different from himself. With his admission I felt a sense of freedom as a cinematographer.

As we began filming, I imagined sometimes Richie was looking over my shoulder, but I had to remind myself of the broad and loosely refined perimeter Richie set early on. What the camera sees is a selective reality through the eye of a cinematographer, only a slice of the whole. Was I able to see what Ritchie experienced? I cannot deny, in any case, that many inspiring photographs or films were lurking in my head, putting a spin on my search for what Ritchie saw and wrote in his journal. At this juncture, over thirty years had passed since I left Japan, my memory of the country was in the distant past, and I felt I was in a relatively neutral state. I could make a stab at capturing visual dramas as Ritchie saw them.

The music of The Inland Sea *was composed by Tōru Takemitsu, one of the major Japanese composers, author among other things of the soundtracks of cult films such as* Empire of Passion *directed by Nagisa Ōshima and* Ran *directed by Akira Kurosawa.*

Composer Toru Takemitsu (*Woman in the Dune, Rising Sun*) made an indelible input in *The Inland Sea*. Sparse but arresting and elegant, his theme music built an eloquent bridge between the words and the pictures; sometimes its variations were repeated in different parts of the film, as if recalling Richie's presence, his sentiment. Takemitsu said he welcomed ethnic musical instruments from remote lands when they roused compelling emotions consonant with his own. I believe his music in turn spoke to people across borders. Later I found out that Takemitsu and Isamu Noguchi were good friends, and he said of Noguchi (I came upon his quote while making *Isamu Noguchi: Stones and Paper*), "when Noguchi returned from his travel from exotic places and told me his experience, it expanded the geography of my mind." I can see them sharing so much in common, exploring the unfamiliar with wonderment, though their creations were in a very different vein.

hollywood

The Inland Sea's frame

Did you already know Richie?

I only knew of Richie through his books. We started the film with an interview with him (for the archives) with him reviewing his original journal of *The Inland Sea* in his apartment in Tokyo. We also filmed him strolling in his neighborhood, his adopted home. An auspicious start to get to know him, I thought, but we never saw him again. I believe he intended to let the filmmakers experience the journey on their own. A few years later he wrote me–I was very surprised to hear from him–saying I was the right cinematographer to film his journal.

What about the choice of shooting in black and white and in color?

Carra wanted Richie and the present day filmed in black & white and his journey in color, contrary to the usual construct. I think it was a thoughtful idea. In color, Richie's journey came alive and intimate. Yet, layered over the images, his own narrative voice echoed the bygone time.

Did you shoot on regular 16mm film with the intent to blow up to 35mm at 1:66?

It did not occur to me that the film would be blown up to 35mm eventually for film festival circuits. I did not film it in super 16mm because that eliminated 16mm release prints with the optical sound track area taken away by the image. But the 35mm blow-up turned out fairly acceptable. With 4K digital the quality now is so much better.

The sequence on the leper island is really memorable. What do you remember about shooting this?

As sensitive as the facility was, we were given permission to film on the tiny island if we only took wide shots, people in the distance, refraining from showing the victims' disfigurement. Yet there was no inspector following and keeping an eye on us, and Carra would tell me or point out to me the images she wanted to capture. We saw several elderly people with bandaged hands–probably missing or degenerating fingers–playing a croquet game on a field, and I took some wide shots first, then went ahead and took tighter shots hoping they were not offensive. They kept on playing the game as if we were not in their view, and engaged in lively conversation amongst themselves. Likewise, we captured any images that showed how the leprosy victims coped with adverse isolation on the island, just a stone's throw away from society across the water.

You oversaw the restored 4K digital transfer in 2019, for The Criterion Collection. How did you do it?

I had a telephone conversation with the timer and explained which scenes–very few–needed improvement as the original DVD release was acceptable in general. I received a copy of his first color grading and I was very satisfied. I would have preferred to sit with the timer and supervise the color grading, but I was impressed with the result expedited through telephone conversation. A sign of evolving technology.

hollywood

Have you often returned to Japan?

The last time I went to Japan was in 1997 to film *Isamu Noguchi: Stones & Paper*. Most of my immediate relatives are now gone in Japan and I have not had another opportunity go there in recent years.

The second work with Carra was Dvořák and America, *the first U.S./Czech Television documentary co-production. It is the first film about the years the composer Antonín Dvořák spent in the United States teaching at the National Conservatory of Music of New York. The cinematographers are Antonín Chundela, Allen Moore and you: for New York and the Midwest?*

Dvorak wrote some of the best-known chamber music in the US. My brief filming was in Iowa, in a small community where Dvorak spent time with his family among Czech immigrants. Today the community proudly safeguards the mementos from Dvorak's brief stay. Carra and I traced Dvorak's steps.

What can you tell me about your collaboration with Carra?

For *The Inland Sea* Carra had spent months in Japan preparing before filming began, and she knew the area like her own backyard. During her research she found some of the people who paralleled in spirit what Richie encountered and aptly described in his journal; he said they are close to the Mediterranean by nature, open and less self-conscious than those in the cities. Isolated from the mainland by the sea, the passage of time has had little effect on their lives. The fashion might have changed, maybe there are more cars on the street. When the camera was pointed at people, they seemed oblivious of it, in spite of some non-Japanese members in the crew. They were nonchalant or even accommodating to our filming. It made my work much freer and more intimate... Carra gave me a range of freedom, to be inquisitive as any cinematographer would be, but with simplicity and clarity. And if

hiro narita. depth of field

any image could say a lot, she welcomed it. She also described to me certain images she had in her mind, however modern they appeared, that reflected Richie's experience decades ago, the moments of his personal encounters as if they are today. And we found many in *The Inland Sea*.

You worked also with the director Richard Donner on Tales from the Crypt - episode Showdown *(1992). He directed films such as* Superman, The Goonies, Scrooged, *and the* Lethal Weapon *series.*

The *Tales from the Crypt* series produced by HBO were released by censorship from network standards and practices. Many prominent directors and actors, for this very reason, volunteered to showcase their work in the series. I took part in *Showdown*, a western ghost story directed by Richard Donner (*Lethal Weapon*). It was an invigorating shoot with Donner's exuberance and abundant experience. I, too, was motivated and challenged in my own craft.

Can you describe any sequence that satisfied you most?

In the saloon scene, a dozen ghosts of murdered cowboys surround the accused murderer–a ghost himself now. The key light source came from two windows, which I decided to cover with old newspapers hiding the green lawn and the trees of the studio lot seen through them. Two HMIs blasted through each window from outside and I kept the fill-light to bare minimum. Of course, the newspapers were overexposed and illegible, giving the appearance of dirty windows. The result was an eerie interior with the actors becoming ghostly figures, their faces highlighted only by the window but the rest of the details was compressed and indistinct. A bit of ambience smoke added to the effect. And there were other images in this short film I was very proud of.

Showdown *is written by Frank Darabont: as a director, he is known for his film adaptations of Stephen King novellas and nov-*

els such as The Shawshank Redemption *(1994)*, The Green Mile *(1999)*.

I don't recall meeting him during the production.

Hocus Pocus is a 1993 American fantasy comedy film directed by Kenny Ortega. Main roles were performed by Bette Midler, Sarah Jessica Parker, Kathy Najimy. The film shows a terrifying comic trio of witches. Hocus Pocus *was the first Disney production to use digital visual effects?*

If I remember, digital visual effects were in the early stage of development. Miniature puppets, and rear-view projection were still the main tools used in this film. Perhaps, digital scanning and compositing replaced optical scanning in the film, eliminating the use of the 8-perf large format camera to compensate for image degradation. We did shoot one scene of the three witches flying together against a green screen because it was physically impractical to shoot outdoors.
The witches flying through the forest were suspended by cables as in the case of *The Rocketeer*. On this movie Disney was very safety conscious for the actors and told us to increase the thickness of the wires. Fortunately, the tree branches on the stage blurred them out, and very little wire-removal treatment was necessary.

What kind of lighting did you choose for this story?

The story takes place during the Halloween holiday, the time of harvest, and pumpkin is predominant used as decoration for the occasion. I was mindful of this festive color, orange, to be incorporated into the lighting scheme. There is a musical scene (I'll Put a Spell on You) performed by the three witches at a Halloween party, showcasing Bette Midler's musical virtuosity. I suggested to the producer to hire a professional stage lighting person to pitch in. He said this scene is not a Broadway revue, it is more like a community effort and I should come up with a lighting design.

Hiro Narita and Bette Midler on the movie set *Hocus Pocus* (1993) directed by Kenny Ortega.

"*Thank you, Hiro – It was a wonderful experience working with you – your*

Director Kenny Ortega was of the same opinion. I understood their concept but I felt it should not be too amateurish for my own sake. After seeing the rehearsal, my gaffer Rao (*Star Trek VI*), the computer dimmer board operator Jeff During (*The Rocketeer*) and I improvised what I felt an exciting, uninhibited solution to complement the performance. As it turned out During, always quiet in his demeanor, was an aficionado of music. and he had an innate sense of rhythm, harmonizing the lighting cues with the music And he made many good suggestions. Our combined ad hoc effort was surprisingly jovial and the result was scintillating. The scene is still shown on YouTube as a music video!

Gunmen is a 1993 action-comedy film directed by Deran Sarafian. It stars Mario Van Peebles, Christopher Lambert, Denis Leary, Kadeem Hardison, and Patrick Stewart.

Impressed by his performance in *Greystoke: The Legend of Tarzan*, I was happy to work on *Gunmen*, an action filled movie. Jalisco, Mexico, was the location during its dry season providing a unique landscape and atmosphere; an addition to my visual lexicon. Lambert enjoyed and played the comedic role with energy. And I was surprised to see Patrick Stewart in the cast playing a rogue boss in a wheelchair. He was by then getting great notice as Captain Picard in the *Star Trek: Next Generation* series, but at the time I was ignorant of his background, a remarkable accomplishment in the Royal Shakespeare Company (Laurence Olivier Award, 1979). Playing a villain in the film, my respect for his professionalism grew.

Deran Sarafian is the son of the director Richard C. Sarafian, author of the film Vanishing Point *(1971). He is also the nephew of Robert Altman.*

Richard Sarafian played a police chief in *Gunman* and I knew of him as a wonderful actor and the director of *Vanishing Point*. I had no idea he was related to Robert Altman.

hiro narita. depth of field

Long Shadows *(1994)* a TV film directed by Sheldon Larry is based on the life of Japanese-born, American-educated author Haru Matsukata who married U.S. ambassador to Tokyo Edwin O. Reischauer, played by Fumi Dan and Matt Frewer respectively. What can you tell me: did you know their story?

Born in Japan and educated at Harvard, Edwin Reischauer was a well-respected scholar of Asian history and when he became the US ambassador to Japan, he was greeted like a movie celebrity, married to a Japanese woman. I knew at least that much before the filming. As I worked on the film, I learned that he was a very influential figure behind the scenes in rebuilding the relationship between post-war Japan and the US. Fumi Dan, a popular Japanese actress with basic English, played his wife Haru and learned the English dialogue phonetically; we were very impressed. The story covered a long span of time; Haru's life during the war, her marriage to Reischauer (Matt Frewer), his ambassadorship, and their later life in the US. It was both a challenging and inspiring historical drama to film. In Los Angeles, Reischauer's widow visited us and loaned us as film props many of the household items she and her husband used. It was a very touching moment. Frewer (*Honey, I Shrunk the Kids*) nearly unrecognizable from our previous work together, loved his very first trip to Japan.

You also worked in Las Vegas, taking care of the cinematography for the show Siegfried & Roy: The Magic and Mystery *(1994) directed by Charles A. Bangert. Siegfried & Roy were a duo of German-American magicians and entertainers. It was composed of Siegfried Fischbacher and Roy Horn. In their show, the magicians incorporated a menagerie of magical beasts—including white tigers, lions and elephants. These two are the original Tiger Kings. Siegfried brought the magic and Roy brought animal expertise. Together they created one of the most popular shows that ever ran on the Las Vegas Strip.*

hollywood

This television special about the life of the very popular magician duo and their performance in Las Vegas was a unique experience, not particularly from cinematographic standpoint, but from understanding how magic and illusion are created as a misdirection of our grasp of reality at any given moment. And I realized our ability to see is tenuous and even imperfect under certain circumstances. Curiously, I felt its survival might be necessary part of being human.

The beginning of the show is set in a fantastic snowy world, far away from time ... where did you shoot?

The sequence at night with the white tiger in the snow was filmed at a ski resort near Las Vegas, a place where you hardly imagine snow would be present. On the night of the shoot, however, we had to bring in a snow machine to replenish the snow, keeping the area fully blanketed.

Hiro Narita with Siegfried & Roy

What memory do you have of them?

I realized that a magic show depends heavily on misdirection, optical illusion and timely execution. Some tricks were deceptively obvious and we had to sign a non-disclosure agreement to prevent the magic formula from leaking to the public. Above all, magic or not, Siegfried and Roy practiced their acts daily as athletes do; to keep fit; Siegfried's dexterity with his hands and Roy's gymnastic ability were central to their performance. I became unsettlingly aware of the flaws in our cognition. Our ability to "follow through" an event is easily confused and derailed by small distractions, diversions. It was a fascinating revelation. The breathtaking animals' presence added in swaying our focus. To film the show, I had to depend on the basic stage lighting already designed and choreographed with the visual spectacle and extravaganza; all essential elements of their show. We also filmed them experimenting with new magic acts on stage without an audience. Allowing us to film their acts only from the front, "audience perspective", was a crucial condition to achieve optimum illusions. Our film also included their daily life at home. Situated adjacent to the house were quarters for tigers, lions, and a few other animals and the caretakers. I saw the animals roaming around in the yard like domesticated pets. Siegfried and Roy, being gracious and accommodating hosts, opened their home to us unveiling their life and their living motto; the magic and the miracle.

Are you fascinated by magic and these kinds of shows?

I've always loved magic. I was particularly fascinated by how these tricks were achieved. By diverting our attention for an instant, some tricks, even seen at close proximity, left me baffled. Our perception, I've come to suspect and admit, is erratic and vulnerable to manipulation. A magician directs our attention to what he wants us to see in a certain way, and we are easily swayed. I wonder if it happens in our daily activity? But this may not be so harmful, and may even be necessary at times, in our

hollywood

survival mechanism; not noticing everything around us. We may already be living with magic.

You worked (as additional cinematographer) with Zara Muren, director of the documentary Dream of the Sea Ranch *(1994) about Sea Ranch, the acclaimed residential development in Northern California, which includes interviews with developer/architect Al Boeke, landscape architect Lawrence Halprin, and architects Joseph Esherick and Charles Moore. What memories do you have?*

I met Zara through her husband Dennis Muren (*Star Wars, Jurassic Park*) and she asked me if I would film the houses at the Sea Ranch for her documentary film in progress. The architectural designs at the Ranch were innovative and progressive, receiving much attention from colleagues and the public. I had seen the initial stage in the mid-60s and admired the designs integrating the surroundings and making the utmost use of natural elements: the sun, the wind, and the Pacific Ocean shoreline. I enthusiastically joined her project and filmed the houses showcasing their distinctive design features. Zara is a landscape architect herself and a documentary filmmaker, and she had been compiling interviews with noted architects all over the world–the interviews in the film are from her own archives–and The *Dream of the Sea Ranch* is the epitome of her professional interest.

Lawrence Halprin is Daria's father, did you know him?

I was working with a studio that was collaborating in designing signs for the Sea Ranch project in which Halprin had a big role as a landscape architect. So, he visited the studio periodically to check on the progress, and I met him there. It is the very same studio where I met John Korty and decided to take the production assistant job on his first feature film.

Zara is the wife of Dennis Muren who won nine Oscars in total: eight for Best Visual Effects and a Technical Achievement

hiro narita. depth of field

Academy Award. He is the Senior Visual Effects Supervisor and Creative Director of Industrial Light & Magic. You have worked together in some films, what can you tell me about him?

With all his pioneering and creative achievements under his belt, Muren was unassuming and collaborative. Working together on a number of projects, he never showed off, nor did he hesitate to answer my questions or seek my opinions. Inspired by Ray Harryhausen at an early age, Muren's vast contributions to visual effects, from physical to computer generated, have revolutionized and ushered in countless possibilities. When I saw those Oscars in his home, all discreetly bunched together on a bookshelf, it was an amazing sight to gaze upon.

White Fang 2: Myth of the White Wolf is a 1994 American Northern adventure film directed by Ken Olin and starring Scott Bairstow, Alfred Molina, and Geoffrey Lewis. It is a sequel to the 1991 White Fang directed by Randal Kleiser and was released in theaters by Walt Disney Pictures. Were you involved in the making, following your previous experience in Never Cry Wolf I guess?

When the producer asked me to work on the project my immediate reaction was hesitation about doing another animal film in the north. But the story was more about a young man trying to save a native tribe and its land from mining exploitation; and the story attracted me.

With director Ken Olin, did you take references from the previous film with a young protagonist, Ethan Hawke?

The film actually begins with Jack (Ethan Hawke) writing a letter to his friend Henry (the new protagonist in *White Fang 2*) in Alaska to look after the wolf he left behind. That was the only link to the original film, to show the wolf's continuing saga.

So, what can you tell me about this film?

hollywood

The film was very much a Disney formula and, for me, it was a fantasy-adventure aimed especially at a young audience. Seeing no connection or similarity in the story with *Never Cry Wolf*, I decided to get involved.

Although based in Alaska, filming took place entirely in British Columbia, Canada's Metro Vancouver region: exact?

The location was mostly in British Columbia, in or near Vancouver, for logistic convenience. We built a replica of a native village complete with a potlatch house and totems, beautifully executed by the art department. It was, however, a hybrid of Alaskan Indian and North West Canadian Indian, and if you are keen on ethnology, you might have noticed the architecture and the natives' costumes are close to those of the Canadian Indian. In the Disney world, such differences were overlooked or you turned a blind eye to them. We recruited Haida (Canadian Indians) living nearby as extras, some wearing their own costumes. Looking at the authentically constructed, functional village with the help of native artists, the Haida people were so impressed that they wanted to keep it as a memento, if not actually live in it after filming was over. But Disney made us destroy it, unfortunately, for insurance reasons. The production designer Cary White (*Lonesome Dove*) cleverly built the ceiling beams in the main building which I could use as lighting grids; a thoughtful consideration for the gaffers, making lighting much more efficient. After British Colombia, we moved to Colorado Spring, Colorado, to film the raindeer stampede and the final scene of the movie. There the herd was available near the city and spring flowers were in full bloom against the magnificent mountains, providing a picturesque background, nearly undistinguishable from Alaska.

Did you have particular difficulties in filming?

Many stunt works and special effects were involved, but nothing I felt was exceptionally difficult. The only sequence I felt risky was when White Fang swam across a rapid river to save Henry. The trainer brought a specially trained wolf hybrid to swim and a safety net was placed just below the water's surface, hidden from the camera, to prevent him from being swept away. The filming the scene went like clockwork.

James and the Giant Peach *is a 1996 musical fantasy film directed by Henry Selick, it was produced also by Tim Burton and is a combination of live action and stop-motion animation. It stars Richard Dreyfuss (voice), Susan Sarandon (voice), Paul Terry. You worked on the live action segment.*

Based on Roald Dahl's book, the film version consists of live action and stop-motion animation. The live action segment, in which I was involved with actors (Joanna Lumley, Miriam Margolyes, and Paul Terry as James) was entirely filmed on stage in San Francisco. The imaginative and whimsical sets incorporated distorted and forced perspectives. One street set was no more than 100 feet in depth. But with miniature trains running in the background against the buildings, each drastically reduced in size and in depth, the street looked many blocks deep. It was a project full of images as if a children's picture book had come alive.

Did you compare with your colleague Pete Kozachik ASC, who photographed stop motion?

In the very beginning, director Henry Selick (*The Nightmare Before Christmas*) asked me not to consult and exchange ideas with the stop motion director of photography, Pete Kozachik (*The Nightmare Before Christmas*). Rather, Selick preferred us to go creative on our own and he would be the judge and link between the two visual styles. I think he was very wise to do so; the two visual styles did not conflict nor assimilate; instead, they expressed the sum and substance of Dahl's story. I thought computer graphics would expand the scope and dimension of the images, but by staying within the limit of physical sets, as Selik envisioned and which he believed in, the film maintained a fantasy of its own. The stop-motion segment on the other hand created James' magical world stretching to another level, more imaginative and dream-like in scope than the live action.

One large exterior set on the stage was required to be both day and night depending on the scene, and the filming schedule forced us to be flexible enough so that we could switch from day to night and vice-versa at a moment's notice. Again, using the computer-assisted lighting system, I prepared for both situations. That meant hanging more lights and laying extra cables during the rigging. But with the child actor's limited hours of work allowed each day, I could alternate day and night quickly without losing precious time and meet the production schedule. It was, all things considered, a great time-saving and versatile tool.

The film is produced by Tim Burton, did you get to know him? Did he come to the set?

Tim Burton came to the stage just once, when he was escorted to the sets by director Selick. As they inspected, I was introduced to Burton and he welcomed me for joining the project. I thanked him fleetingly, as I did not want to interrupt their conversation.

The Arrival *is a 1996 American-Mexican science fiction horror film written and directed by David Twohy and starring Charlie Sheen: you returned to work with Sheen after* No Man's Land. *Radio astronomer Zane Ziminski (Sheen) works for the S.E.T.I., the NASA program related to the discovery of possible signals of alien origin. What do you remember about this movie?*

I was back at Churubusco Studios and reunited with many of the crew from *Honey, I Shrunk the Kids*, plus Charlie Sheen. In *The Arrival*, the memorable scenes for me dealt with the Day of the Dead parade at night in Taxco, Mexico. Zaminsky (Sheen) bolts out of his house and runs away from an alien chasing after him through a labyrinth of cobblestone streets among the torch-

Hiro Narita and director David Twohy (*The Arrival*, 1995)

Hiro Narita on the movie set *The Arrival* (Mexico)

hollywood

carrying festival procession. The torches helped light the people themselves, augmented by the sparsely placed practical street lights. At the far end of the street, I placed a 5k lamp with an orange jell giving a gleaming backlight to Sheen and the crowd as he runs toward it. Even the light itself was in the frame pointing at the camera, I let it be and hoped that the viewer will not see it as an illogical movie light, but as an otherworldly glow. I think it succeeded. I believe the light, source or ambience, has attributes of its own; it illuminates the physical but expresses the contextual as well.

Visas and Virtue *is a 1997 narrative short film directed by Chris Tashima inspired by the true story of Holocaust rescuer Chiune "Sempo" Sugihara, who is known as "The Japanese Schindler".* Visas and Virtue *won an Academy Award for Live Action Short Film.*

This poignant short story was filmed entirely in Los Angeles substituting for Lithuania and Japan. Bookended by the scene of Sugihara and his wife in their later life (in color) and Sugihara's rescue activities in Lithuania (in black & white), we worked mostly in and around Tashima's parents' house. I guessed the house was built in the 20s and its architecture served perfectly for the Lithuanian home where the Japanese Consulate was situated. In the living room we even built an interior corner of the train compartment assembled from pieces of plywood and painted dark. A pivoting light through the train window–off screen–gave an illusion that the train was slowly departing: such was a simple lighting trick in movie making. The night exterior of the train station, however, was filmed at an outdoor train museum, with many extras dressed as refugees. Sugihara's POV of the refugees from the departing train was a long tracking shot from a dolly, since the train could not be moved.
The volunteers offering their expertise included my regular lighting crew in Hollywood, members of local theaters, and Tashima's family and their friends making lunch; it was truly a joint labor of love.

Tashima's thoughtful staging allowed me to focus on lighting, addressing the haunting moments of the refugees waiting in suspense to receive their visas. Among the extras there was an elderly woman who spoke one line in Japanese to prove she knew Japanese–all applicants had to say it to get a visa. This woman had been an actual recipient of Sugihara's visa, as a young girl: the survivor of his rescue effort!

Visas and Virtue was shot in both color and black and white. What more can you tell me about the cinematography?

Monochromatic photography overcame many imperfections I confronted with the color coordination in the house, the costumes, and even the color temperature of the lights. It was to our advantage in unexpected ways. At the time, my knowledge of black & white photography was limited, but I put aside my inexperience. The monochromatic viewing filter gave me a good parameter of contrast and an approximation of how the color rendered in black & white. My personal understanding of a black and white image is that when it strikes the retina in our eyes it transforms into phantom colors in our brain, integrating with our senses and emotions. As an experiment, if you project three circles of the primary color lights onto a white wall, forming a triangular pattern, the intersection of the three-color space becomes white while the secondary color is produced between the two primaries. Think of a white light passing through our eyes which then is refracted into the spectrum of colors. I believe the prism effect applies to black and white images entering our brain. My unscientific reasoning is that a black and white image does not mean the absence of colors in our perception; our optic sensory system is complex and it is enigmatically linked to the power of our imagination and association.

As mentioned, Visas and Virtue *won the Oscar for Best Live Action Short Film. Did you attend the Oscars awards ceremony?*

hollywood

No, I did not attend the ceremony. I think I was in a production somewhere at the time and I even missed the award ceremony on TV.

World War II is present in some of your works like Farewell to Manzanar *or* Visas and Virtue: *you were just a child, but what do you bring from those years?*

I think you are always part of history; your life is intertwined in it, whether you know it or not. I am sure there were times I steered away from recalling unpleasant memories of war or tried to erase anything in my past that tainted my outlook. But I have come to deal with them in a different perspective. The obstacle courses I have navigated are now "meaningful" experiences; colorful ones at that.
When a script such as *Farewell to Manzanar* was presented to me, depicting racial or political injustices, I had a choice to make; either to take part in it or avoid it. Initially out of curiosity then out obligation, I wanted to be educated on the subject of Japanese American internment during World War II. Then, I felt it important to raise public awareness and share it with others because the historical incident had been reduced to a footnote in the US history. If anything, my personal wartime experiences produced empathy and sympathy toward those who became victims of war. *Visa and Virtues* certainly exemplified my viewpoint.
Furthermore, when I was involved in filming *Go Tell It on The Mountain* (based on James Baldwin's book), I had a glimpse into the racial and social issues veiled in American cultural stigmas. My bold notion was that the movie is a vehicle to explore and instigate such issues beyond being the medium of entertainment.

You mentioned Go Tell It on the Mountain *(1985), the TV movie belonging to the* American Playhouse *series. This film is the adaptation of James Baldwin's celebrated novel. Can you tell me more?*

hiro narita. depth of field

This project came right after working with Gordon Parks and it introduced me to another slice of African-American strife, this time in the early 20th century. I embraced the chance to work on the film adaptation of Baldwin's celebrated novel. The cast consisted entirely of African-American actors, many of them very distinguished; Paul Winfield, Ruby Lee, Alfre Woodard. My first course of action was to attend to the contrast, avoiding placing the actors against a white or bright background or wearing bright clothes. Well, my fear became real; the main living room location in New York–I had no voice in selecting it–had white walls and they could not be painted, at the owner's request. To solve the issue, I had the gaffer hang a black skirt around the ceiling lights to reduce the spill on the walls, but at the same time, keeping enough illumination on the actors. This would have been a routine and easily executed job in a studio, but in the real apartment it turned into a delicate operation. As for the costumes, the veteran costume designer dyed all the white fabric in tea solution so they looked a shade darker but appeared white in the film. In the small church many women wore white head-coverings or hats, or even white dresses which belonged to the extras, and I had to yield to the situation. But in this instance the contrast created images accentuating the ecstatic moments and I welcomed it. From my experience with Parks' film, black actors of varying skin tones were not notably tricky or difficult to light as you might think. If the light source is kept with a warmer color temperature, the skin color was lifted. Cooler key light, I learned, was to be avoided–it seemed to add contrast and darken the skin tone. The earlier part of the story took place in a rural Georgia, and the rest in Harlem, New York in the 20s and the 30s; providing strikingly visual arrays. The inner-city streets and the clothes people wore distinctly captured the depression era and they were very photogenic to my eyes.

The director Stan Lathan has directed pilots for many popular sitcoms... How did you work with him?

Director Lathan–I did not know about him before the project–had directed many television programs of diverse contents. He was, as I understood, involved in the civil rights movement before getting into directing, making a big change in his life.

In the storefront church scene, the churchgoers broke into a hymn and ecstatic dance, some speaking in tongues. Lathan energized the crowd by dancing off camera, displaying his hidden talent. At one point, actor Giancarlo Esposito spoke in tongues in his zest, even collapsing on to the floor in the middle of his act. I don't remember if it was scripted, but the amazing scene carried on. I admired Lathan's energy in orchestrating such a dramatic, spontaneous moment; and I was very moved by the Baldwin's story of the two generations of family in both societal and personal conflicts.

Have you met James Baldwin?

Baldwin lived in France and a few years after the film's broadcast on television he passed away–he might have been ill for a while. I am sorry I did not meet him.

With director Lynn Hershman Leeson you have collaborated on many projects over the span of twenty-five years. In particular I would like to mention three of these starring actress Tilda Swinton.

Conceiving Ada *(1997) is your first film together. Tilda Swinton plays Ada Augusta Byron King, Countess of Lovelace. In this film Bill Zarchy is the cinematographer of virtual sets.*

Lynn Hershman Leeson was already a very accomplished, international groundbreaking artist in many different media: photography, video, installation, and performance. Her first narrative film, *Conceiving Ada,* dealt with a female computer wizard reaching into the past-mid 19th century England–and through virtual reality communicates with Ada Byron Lovelace (Tilda Swinton) who was credited with writing the world's first computer program. The story did not sound pure fantasy or science fiction to me. The virtual world has more pragmatic presence in our life today. By this time, compositing software–still analogue for graphics, photographs, and live actions–became readily available on the consumer market. And Lynn's film student from the University of California, Davis, participated in compositing the actors against the virtual sets (35mm still photos of Victorian interiors taken in San Francisco), to which Hershman Leeson integrated graphics. The protagonist's present day and Ada in Victorian times were filmed in 35mm film, but the scenes with others, including Timothy Leary, in virtual reality were captured in video by videographer Bill Zarchy. Leeson's quest into identity politics and biopolitics, from reality to virtuality, is foremost in her artistic pursuit, and technology and art are intrinsic to her work. Before the project I saw Tilda Swinton in Orlando and was absolutely captivated by her performance, her presence in the film. And to see her in person and work on *Conceiving Ada*, was a dream come through.

Teknolust (2002) *is about the scientist Rosetta Stone (Tilda Swinton) who injects her DNA into three Self-Replicating Automatons (S.R.A.s). Also in the cast is Karen Black, actress of cult films such as* Easy Rider *(1969), directed by and starring Dennis Hopper and* Five Easy Pieces *(1970) directed by Bob Rafelson.*

In *Teknolust*, a bio-geneticist (Swinton) creates three clones of herself, and we filmed it entirely in high-definition, still analogue at the time. Often Swinton's clones appeared in the same frame, sometimes two Swintons and a photo double. We devised very simple compositions where they are spliced together, not requiring complicated compositing. The cast included Karen Black, who played Ada Byron King's mother in *Conceiving Ada* with Swinton, played a detective named Dirty Dick; Hershman Leeson's another muse on identity politics. This project spurred me to be a proponent of high-definition cinematography. The tool had advanced substantially since shooting a demo-film in the

Tilda Swinton on the set of *The Strange Culture*. Photo by Charlie Kuttner

hiro narita. depth of field

Teknolust's frame: Tilda Swinton

mid-80s for Sony's prototype high-definition analogue camera, in collaboration with ILM. At the time, it was very cumbersome with the recording console a size of a refrigerator tethered to the camera with a thick cable. If we unplugged it to reposition the camera beyond the reach of the console, we had to re-calibrate the colors and pixel registration, taking at least half an hour each time. In spite of this, George Lucas, while observing our shoot, was convinced and adamant over thirty years ago that this technology was the future of film making, ushering us on to a new level of visual storytelling.

Strange Culture (2007) *examines the case of artist and professor Steve Kurtz (played by Thomas Jay Ryan), a member of the Critical Art Ensemble (CAE). After his wife, Hope (played by Swinton), died of heart failure, paramedics arrived and became suspicious when they noticed petri dishes and other scientific equipment related to Kurtz's art in his home. They summoned the FBI, who detained Kurtz within hours on suspicion of bioterrorism.*

hollywood

A trailblazer in advocating freedom of expression, Hershman Leeson decided to make a documentary film to challenge the legal issue surrounding artist Steve Kurtz. He had been held under house arrest, accused of being a bio-terrorist because of his work involving biotechnology and ecological struggle. Bio-terrorism was a global fear and Steve Kurtz fell right into the profile. *Strange Culture* consists of archival news footage, interviews, and an enactment of Kurtz (Thomas Jay Ryan) and his wife (Tilda Swinton), which I worked on. It was a blend of narrative and documentary film. At one point in the film, Kurtz himself and the actor portraying him were interviewed together, sitting side by side, blurring the border between the factual and the fictional, the real and the imagined.

What can you tell me about an actress like Tilda? Her performance in Michael Clayton *(2007) won her the Academy Award for Best Supporting Actress and the BAFTA Award for Best Actress in a Supporting Role.*

Swinton was more than a performer; she was an instigator and collaborator in this case with Hershman Leeson's view. On the day of the *Strange Culture* shoot, just arriving from the airport, Swinton was given the script, and in a short time she was ready to act. I am sure she was briefed in advance of Kurtz' circumstance. With her hair finger-combed and with no makeup she proceeded to play Kurtz' wife. I wouldn't call it improvisational; more like instinctual performance. We shot Swinton in one afternoon in Hershman Leeson's apartment, and the next day she presented her state of cinema speech at San Francisco International Film Festival.

For American Masters, *a PBS television series which produces biographies on enduring writers, musicians, visual and performing artists, dramatists, filmmakers, you directed* Isamu Noguchi: Stones and Paper *(1997) that chronicles the life and distinguished career of this world-renowned Japanese-American sculptor. The*

hiro narita. depth of field

profile is narrated by Linda Hunt. How was this experience as a director?

As a child growing up in Japan, I saw Noguchi's work in a magazine and I was captivated by his playful and imaginative creations. Whenever I saw them in my adult life, they triggered my fond memory of my childhood fascination, but with a more matured frame of mind. A friend suggested I should make a documentary film about Noguchi who had passed away ten years earlier, but his work in recent years had rebounded in the art world and was rediscovered by the public. I too began to take notice. The friend also said, since I am bi-cultural my background was suited to tackle the film; the assumption was too simplistic, still, it was an intriguing proposition.

After a long and tedious process of writing a proposal (by producer William Smock) and fund raising, my studio was awarded a grant from the National Endowment for Humanities, and we launched the Noguchi project. As I uncovered Noguchi's six decades of artistic life, as sculptor, landscape architect, and even designer of paper lanterns and furniture, I began to understand and appreciate the journey he took in his long career; from his comprehension of stones having personality to his exploration of the space around them–space being an active and participatory element. I found Noguchi's concept vaguely analogous to filmmaking, though the film is a two-dimensional medium creating three-dimensional psychological space in the viewer's mind.

And this project was my opportunity to integrate graphic design background and cinematography, familiar territories on my part. So, I needed to see his creations through my own eyes. Some limited archival footage of Noguchi, including interviews, were available through private sources. But his former assistant and stone cutter Masatoshi Izumi was still active in Japan and gave us vital information about Noguchi and his many years of working experience with him. As the guardian of Noguchi's studio, Izumi kept it in a pristine condition and I was able to film

Noguchi's studio and his work as if he had just stepped out. Visiting Noguchi Garden Museum (located in Takamatsu, Japan, facing the Inland Sea), the counterpart to The Noguchi Museum in New York, I saw his works were deeply rooted and belonged to where they stood, at home in their environment.

Why did you choose to make a documentary about this artist?

Why did Noguchi's work fascinate me in my childhood? The deeper our research dug in, the more I was moved by his principles, and my interest broadened beyond just curiosity. Noguchi said, he cannot be by himself all the time, he must go out; but he cannot be out all the time, he must come back to himself to find the source of his expression. His quest to reach out and reach in was the undercurrent I began to understand and identify.
A child born out of wedlock, Noguchi's Japanese father left him and his American mother when he was still young. Following ever-shifting paths, Noguchi moved to New York, then to France to become an apprentice with Brancusi. I recognized a little bit of Noguchi in those of us in artistic pursuit through twists and turns, in search of connections in all things seen and unseen. For me, this project became clear and important when I saw Noguchi's footprints around me.

Why did you choose Linda Hunt as the narrator?

We thought of Peter Coyote (*E.T., The Blue Yonder*) as narrator at one point. But we felt his voice was too recognizable. The producer then suggested Linda Hunt. I loved the idea; her voice was recognizable by many in PBS programs, but her shade of deep and solemn voice–a voice of the cultivated–I thought was unique and perfect for Noguchi. Hunt accepted our request instantly, and importantly, she was familiar with Noguchi's work. The only condition she stipulated was that we record her in a small studio walking distance from her house in Los Angeles, an easy request to fulfill.

hiro narita. depth of field

In your "Isamu Noguchi" also appears the well-known artist Christo - stage name of the Bulgarian sculptor Christo Javachev (Gabrovo 1935 - New York 2020). He is considered one of the most significant exponents of land art and is known in particular for his projects and executions of "packaging" famous public and natural scenery.

The interviews with Christo, also with I.M. Pei, were added as an afterthought in the film, suggested by the academic consultants on the film to boost the film with internationally known artists and Noguchi's friends. As I was in the middle of editing, I sent my producer to film them, and regrettably, I had no contact with Christo.

Have you ever thought about directing a fiction film?

A few times in my career I pondered directing narrative films. And some friends also brought me similar questions. I observed that directing requires a special ability to communicate with actors, not simply engage in cursory talks, and the director remains focused on storytelling; its content, composition, and structure. Of course, a director must have a strong desire to tell the story, navigating through a myriad of negotiations behind the camera to realize his aspiration. In these aspects, knowing my weakness in verbal and literary skill, I had second thoughts and decided to remain in a collaborative role as cinematographer, which in itself is inspiring and gratifying.

I'll Be Home for Christmas *is a 1998 American Christmas family comedy film directed by Arlene Sanford, with Jonathan Taylor Thomas and Jessica Biel. What do you remember about this film?*

A challenging part of this project was capturing the changing climate from warm California to winter on the East Coast of the US, since it was all filmed during spring in California and British Columbia (substituting the East Coast). This meant the special effects crew in Canada had to create artificial snow-covered streets, trees, and houses, even with some residual snows in places. Since computer graphics were not allocated in the budget, we had to live with the condition set on us, mainly using tons of paper-snow. Thankfully it did not melt while we spent many days filming; besides, it was biodegradable if left and abandoned on streets.

At the time, a very young Jessica Biel was among the interpreters (as Mary Camden) of the family drama series 7th Heaven, that she would later leave to devote herself completely to cinema with titles like The Rules of Attraction, The Illusionist, Next, Total Recall, Hitchcock, *becoming one of the most famous actresses in Hollywood. What do you remember about her? She played Allie.*

I knew Jessica Biel was from the popular TV series *7th Heaven*. Beyond that, I knew very little about her career, and to me she was just a member of the cast in the film at the time. A few years later her name and photos were popping up in the Hollywood Reporter and trade magazines, her popularity surging quickly. I almost did not recognize her because she had grown so much in a few years.

Shadrach *(1998) was directed by Susanna Styron, a film based on a short story by her father William Styron, starring Harvey Keitel and Andie MacDowell. In* Shadrach *you dispensed with any hint of sepia tone, which is often used when lighting such period films. Also, you used naturalism in lighting. The source of light, especially on interiors, needed to seem to come from natural, logical places or windows, right?*

A touching story of reconciliation between a former slave and the descendent of the family who owned him. It was filmed in North Carolina. I felt strongly, as director Styron agreed, that images should render a simplicity of natural rural life, without embellishment. In the interior of a house, for example, if the window was the key source of light, I augmented the ambience with lights bouncing off the walls or the floor, and quite often, off a piece of card painted in color similar to the surrounding. In reality, the color temperature of ambience varies depending on where you are in a room. The light from a window facing north is cooler (higher units in Kelvins) than a window facing south. By mixing the color temperatures, I was able to render the atmosphere as close to natural as I saw, and get enough exposure for the high-speed negative film. Sometimes, I imagined a window where there was none, or blocked excessive light from unwanted ones. I took license to maintain simplicity. I believe Nestor Almendros was a master at this. The confining interior rooms–we did not build any set–forced me to stay within the boundary of reality. We were so accustomed to moving walls to get better camera angles in studio sets. In spite of logistical inconveniences, and because of the limitations brought on camera positions, we captured the spaces as they really were.

You remembered Nestor Almendros ASC, master of natural light. He won the Academy Award for Best Cinematography for Days of Heaven (1978) directed by Terrence Malick. *Do you have any memories of him? Have you ever met?*

When *Days of Heaven* was released in 1978 it was an eye opener to many of us aspiring cinematographers. Malick's and Almendros's images took naturalism to another level, to the ethereal realm. I was really moved. From French New Wave on, Almendros' work inspired me deeply and, I wish I had met him and asked him questions about filming *Sophie's Choice* based on William Styron's book.

Andie MacDowell was famous at the time for such films as Sex, Lies, and Videotape *(1989),* Green Card *(1990) and* Four Weddings and a Funeral *(1994).*

Andie MacDowell (born and raised in South Carolina and speaking the regional dialect), with whom we were familiar as an elegant, glamorous actress, wore a plain dress devoid of make-up, became a real country dweller, naturally integrating into the environment. I thought her performance was one of her best. By the way, *Sex, Lies, and Video Tape* was photographed by my former assistant cameraman Walter Lloyd. I was glad to see him advancing in his career.

In Shadrach, *Harvey Keitel plays the part of Vernon Dabney. He has starred in films such as* Mean Streets, Taxi driver, The Duelists, Pulp Fiction, The Piano. *What was it like working with him?*

To be honest, I did not know what to expect of him. I had seen his powerful performances in several of Scorsese's films and in *The Piano* by Jane Campion, a very contrasting act, displaying a wide range in his talent. With this seasoned actor, I anticipated, sooner or later, there would be spirited and animated exchange of opinions with director Styron (this was her directorial debut), but to my relief he never showed any contentious behavior on set. As an experienced actor Keitel was keenly aware of the camera position, but he knew when to play to it or not play to it. This reminded me of Kurosawa saying he uses a B camera often so that when the actor plays consciously towards the A camera, the B camera often gets better shots because he is not self-conscious as to how he should be photographed. Keitel frequently gave us both A and B camera angles in one take. His experience was enormously helpful.

Have you met William Styron? Did he come to visit the set?

In spite of some limitations I faced, this is one of my favorite films, seemingly simplistic on the surface but more poignant than meet the eye. One day William Styron (author of *Sophie's Choice*) visited the set to give support to his daughter's effort and to lend his impartial encouragement to all those involved in transforming his short story into a feature film. The director disclosed to me that her father overheard a conversation in a bar which he developed it into the soul-stirring chapter Shadrack in the collection of short stories, *A Tidewater Morning.*

The film is narrated by Martin Sheen. Did you see each other again after the Apocalypse Now *experience or was there no chance?*

The narration was recorded long after the filming and I did not see him.

The film's producers also include Oscar-winning director Jonathan Demme. Have you met him?

Jonathan Demme sent a message wishing us good luck on the first day of the shooting. Styron read it to the crew; a great gesture, but we did not see him during production.

Simon Birch *is a 1998 American comedy-drama film loosely based on the 1989 novel* A Prayer for Owen Meany *by John Irving and written for the screen and directed by Mark Steven Johnson in his directorial debut, starring Ian Michael Smith, Joseph Mazzello, Ashley Judd, Oliver Platt and Jim Carrey as Adult Joe Wenteworth / Narrator. You worked on this film as a cinematographer's second unit. What do you remember about this movie?*

The scene of the school bus partially submerged in a lake and the passengers being rescued from it was filmed in an outdoor swimming pool in Los Angeles. The wide shot, snow in place, had been already filmed in Canada and we had to recreate and match it for details with the actors. I had a large silk tent built over the pool to maintain the overcast weather of the first unit shoot. Some underwater photography was involved, luckily in warm southern California.

Dirty Pictures *is a 2000 American docudrama directed by Frank Pierson. The movie focuses on the 1990 trial of Cincinnati Contemporary Arts Center director Dennis Barrie, who was accused of promoting pornography. The actor James Woods plays the role of Barrie. With this film you received your second Primetime Emmy Awards nomination. What do you remember about the movie?*

Paradoxically, *Dirty Pictures* could not be made in the US without legal arbitration due to Robert Mapplethorpe's controversial photographs. Curator Dennis Barrie (James Woods) and the Cincinnati Center were acquitted on obscenity charges, but filming it was another issue. Instead, it was filmed in Toronto, Canada, a city more tolerant of freedom of expression. The actual Mapplethorpe photographs titled The Perfect Moment, comprised of sadomasochistic images, celebrity portraits (including that of Noguchi), and still lifes, were shipped to Toronto labeled as movie props to avoid attention by border inspection.

How was your collaboration with Frank Pierson? He was also a great screenwriter, even winning an Oscar for the film Dog Day Afternoon *(1975) directed by Sidney Lumet.*

Frank Pierson encouraged me to be bolder and graphic in lighting. For a television film (*Showtime*) it was a welcoming chance to go beyond the normal visual latitude; food for thought as a cinematographer. I am sure he wanted the movie to reflect some aspects of Mapplethorpe's sense of graphics, of his aesthetic, as I too saw in his work. During the location scout, Pierson described me his plan for each scene. On the day of shooting, as actors rehearsed, I focused my attention on their blocking; where they position themselves in relation to their environment, geography. It was important for me to see first the mood and atmosphere in which the scene unfolds. In that sense I light the set first, and see where the actors place themselves. If an actor is not in the light but the tenor of his character at that moment is captured, I leave it as is. But if he needs a delineation, an emphasis, I add a light to dramatize it, adjusting it accordingly. This was more or less my approach to the film.

hiro narita. depth of field

Can you give me some information about the locations?

A generic courtroom set was available in the city and the basic lights were already in place. Making modifications for the film–I chose to make it late afternoon–was relatively uncomplicated. I did not use most of the preinstalled overhead lights for ambience. I was aware that the actual trial went on for weeks, if not months–in the film the trial in progress was intermittently cut into the story–but I kept the lighting very consistent throughout the film as if it took place in one afternoon, to sustain the ongoing trial and the emotional drama intact, unbroken. Using the windows as the source of light, in general, I left the courtroom spectators in the shadow. The museum photo gallery was built in a warehouse space–I am not sure if it was modeled on the actual location–I kept it subdued with a spot light on each photograph.

What memories do you have of Woods?

During the project James Woods was always in lively conversation with someone around him when the camera was not rolling, involving a wide range of subjects, and I particularly enjoyed eavesdropping on his steady streams of discussion with the director.

In Dirty Pictures *Susan Sarandon and Salman Rushdie played the role of themselves. Do you remember their appearance?*

The interviews with the celebrities were video-taped in a small studio in New York. I was awestruck by the lineup of well-known figures like Sarandon and Rushdie, in addition to William Buckley (political commentor) and Barney Frank (US House of Representative), who were prominent in the public media and politics. Pierson scheduled the interviews so that the participants did not meet each other and exchange opinions on Mapplethorpe before we taped them. I was tempted to have a conversation with some of them on more personal interests, but I refrained–as I customarily do with actors–intruding on their moments of concentration.

San Francisco

2000s-2010s

Fortress 2: Re-Entry *(2000) is a science fiction action film directed by Geoff Murphy and stars Christopher Lambert. It is the sequel to 1992's* Fortress, *again played by Lambert and directed by Stuart Gordon.*

It was my second opportunity to work with Christopher Lambert, once in Mexico, and this time in Luxembourg. His professionalism and friendly attitude were always positive on the set and toward the crew. The crew was assembled from several European countries; the art department from the UK, the lighting crew from Denmark–with ingenious clips and clamps which were becoming popular in the US– and the camera operator Alessandro Bolognesi and his assistant Maurizio Cremisini from Italy. The camera crew had worked with me before on *Sub Down*, also filmed in Luxembourg, and I trusted their skill and, importantly, their enthusiasm. I enjoyed the international atmosphere. At the time, Luxembourg was a mini-center of film production in Europe (granting generous tax rebate), and a constant stream of independent and international co-productions were taking place. One day I spotted Rutger Hauer (*Blade Runner*) in the cafeteria enjoying his lunch break alone.

How did you work with New Zealand filmmaker Murphy?

Director Geoff Murphy (*Utu, The Quiet Earth*) was always well-prepared, carring a notebook full of annotations, but he welcomed suggestions from the crew. I had seen his films including his second unit direction on *Dante's Peak*, which required colossal setups and visual effects in creating an aftermath of volcanic devastations. *Fortress 2* might have been relatively easy project for him, but it still required big sets which Murphy handled with ease. I was truly impressed with his quiet composure and diligence. There was another chance to work with him later, but I was already committed to a project and the prospect, to my disappointment, slipped away from me.

The Time Machine (2002) is a science fiction film loosely adapted from the 1895 novel of the same name by H. G. Wells, directed by Simon Wells. Donald McAlpine ACS/ASC was the cinematographer. You worked on film as additional cinematography? Which filming did you take care of? What do you remember about this film?

The 2nd unit director Greg Michael and I worked on the scenes where Alexander (Guy Pearce) along with Eloi are hunted in the bamboo forest by the underground creatures, the Morlocks. They reach the windmill tower and the battles ensue. During the action sequence, we had enormous number of stunt actions and special effects as well as visual effects. And Michael, an experienced director of such elaborate actions, was in charge of the entire segment and we did not have to match anything to the first unit work. I am sure Michael had extensive preliminary discussions with Simon Wells before we started our unit. Donald McAlpine designed silk frames of 40x40 foot and 20x20 foot, suspended overhead by two giant construction cranes so that the bamboo forest was kept in the shade at all times, maintaining the dusk timeline in the story. My lighting crew from *Star Trek VI* provided the necessary lights on the ground and my gaffer kept communications with the crane operators and guided them to reposition the silks as the sun shifted.
Before my shooting began, McAlpine invited me once to a screening of dailies and explained to me his basic approach to the film.

Steve Mathis, now a regular gaffer for McAlpine, supplied me with additional tips I needed. When my unit commenced, I believe McAlpine was filming night scenes and we had no further opportunity to meet and discuss. Not having our segment to intercut directly with the first unit work, my goal was to maintain the dusk. I knew McAlpine would make appropriate color adjustments when his final color grading took place. After the bamboo forest, Michael and I went on to film several pick-ups from other scenes, in which I had to study and recreate the original lighting. We also filmed bits and pieces of the time machine against a green screen, some with Pearce operating it.

Are you fascinated by the idea of being able to travel through time?

My fascination is that time may be nonlinear; past, present, and future are occurring simultaneously, and time as we understand it may be a human concept. Physics and metaphysics are very interesting fields and I enjoy reading them occasionally; they continue to intrigue me.

Also, on The Scorpion King *(2002) an action-adventure fantasy film directed by Chuck Russell, you are accredited as additional cinematographer. Cinematography by John R. Leonetti ASC...*

To be a second or additional unit cinemaphotographer and, for that matter, having a second unit cinematographer in my own project, good understanding must be established with each other and trust in each other's work. I refrained from controlling my second unit cinematographers because they may have something new to contribute. Greg Michael was again the second unit director to meet the challenges on *The Scorpion King* and we spent weeks on new or revised scenes. One scene involved an enormously high and deep greenscreen occupying an entire studio, where the King (Dwayne Johnson/Rock) jumps off a tall tower and lands on a roof below. We worked with both Rock and his stunt/photo double. There was another big scene in a market with

hiro narita. depth of field

The Scorpion King: actor Dwayne "The Rock" Johnson and Hiro Narita (2nd unit)

Rock and many extras in a melee, but I think it was a reshoot of a scene already filmed but later rewritten, and I was not required to match the lighting by the first unit.

Anger Management *(2003) is a dark comedy film directed by Peter Segal and starring Adam Sandler, Jack Nicholson, Marisa Tomei, Woody Harrelson, and John Turturro. In this film you are credited as additional cinematography. Again, with Donald McAlpine ASC's cinematography...*

Donald McAlpine recommended me to the director for filming pick-ups, a large greenscreen shot, and–the biggest part of my assignment–aerial shots approaching and flying over Shea Stadium in New York during an actual night baseball game. In the stadium, at the same time, the first unit was filming the spectators with some actors mingled in. I also did aerial shots of the picture car over Manhattan exiting the city and arriving in Boston. I had not done such extensive aerial photography in the past–except some during *Never Cry Wolf* and *The Candidate*–and I worried that I would be overcome with airsickness. Somehow, I survived without incident with the help of an acupressure wrist band. The helicopter pilot and the camera operator were very experienced, and familiar with the city's strict and complicated new air space ordinance since the 9/11 disaster.

You are also credited as a second unit director...

The directors' guild required a director on such assignments but I felt I could handle it myself. The producer assured he would pay the initiation fee to the guild if I joined. Thinking of possible work in the future on second unit I joined the guild and proceeded to take on the assignments.

The Darwin Awards *is a 2006 American adventure comedy film, based on the website of the same name, written and directed by Finn Taylor. In the movie he stars in addition to Joseph Fiennes, Winona Ryder, David Arquette, Juliette Lewis, Chris Penn, also in a cameo Lawrence Ferlinghetti.*

Based on the real, preposterous, and strange things people do as if they are regressing in human evolution–whence the ironic title *The Darwin Awards*–is a collection of these accounts. Originally, one segment of the film was meant to be video recordings of a crime captured by an off-screen character. As the director planned, we filmed the segment in 16mm instead of video camera for the sake of image quality. Director Taylor later had a change of mind in the editing and he decided to cut some portion of the 16mm footage into the scenes already shot in 35mm. Unexpected and at a loss for words, I had to get informed advice from the local lab I was dealing with. The lab had recently installed a new digital color timing console which, in addition to color grading, facilitated contrast adjustment, grain reduction, and image sharpening. Amazingly, after much tweaking and refining–a technological marvel–many shots came out surprisingly compatible to the 35mm footages, if not to trained eyes.

hiro narita. depth of field

What do you remember about the great American poet, painter, social activist, and co-founder of City Lights Booksellers & Publishers? Lawrence Ferlinghetti, with his own publishing house, published the first literary works of the Beat Generation, including Jack Kerouac and Allen Ginsberg.

City Lights bookstore was one of the locations in the film. Ferlinghetti and City Lights were icons we all knew. Situated only ten minutes' walk from my school I used to visit the bookstore and browsed in the basement full of art history and cinema books on display. I did not fully appreciate the store as the epicenter or crossroads for writers and artists of the beat generation. I just went there because it was a casual and quiet store, packed with books in a maze of narrow aisles. One can spend hours in the basement; mismatched chairs and tables provided a comfortable escape. I had seen Ferlinghetti occasionally for his poetry readings upstairs, but regrettably, I did not attend even once. His popularity spread over several generations, and when he read his poems at *The Last Waltz* to the hearty audience, he received very enthusiastic applause, evidence of his iconic stature in our culture.

The musical group Metallica appears in the film, performing with the song Sad but True. *What can you tell me about their segment?*

In another segment, director Tayler coordinated with the members of Metallica, determining when the singers react to the accident off-screen and deliver the lines in the midst of their live performance. There was only one chance to capture the moment without interrupting their performance. Fortunately, everything went accordingly, and we filmed with multiple cameras. I do not remember if the audience was told in advance of our filming for the movie.

*The actor Chris Penn (*The Wild Life, Reservoir Dogs, The Funeral, Footloose*) - his older brother is Sean Penn - died on January*

24, 2006, the day before the film's premiere at the Sundance Film Festival. Do you remember that sad episode?

I remember the incident, but I had to rifle through my memory to realize which was Sean Penn's brother. He looked very healthy when we filmed him, and I could not imagine he would die so young.

Do you have any particular anecdote about the making of the film?

In addition to filming in and around the landmark City Lights bookstore there was a short scene in which Ryder's and *Fiennes*' characters meet Ferlinghetti at Tosca Café–a Mecca for people in the literary and entertainment world–just across from the bookstore. It turns out Ryder, her parents, and Ferlinghetti had known each other for a long time in literary circles. And when we filmed the scene at the cafe many people in the film business mysteriously showed up for drink and casual conversation, including director Philip Kaufman. Gossip spread like wildfire.

Thanks to Valley of the Heart's Delight *(2006) directed by Tim Boxell, you won the Boston International Film Festival (Best Cinematography). The film is set in idyllic 1933 San Jose, California, where a young reporter tries to save two innocent men from being hanged for murder.*

By the time this project began high-def photography became fully digital and the dynamic range expanded, producing superior color latitude and resolution.
Loosely based on a real event set in the mid-1930s, a young newspaper reporter witnesses a grim, public lynching orchestrated by the owner of the newspaper publisher (Pete Postlethwaite) he worked for. Toward the end of the film as the plot becomes intense and nightmarish, director Tim Boxell and I decided to drain out the color gradually, and the film ends in almost black and white. But the desaturation was done in post-production because we did

hiro narita. depth of field

Valley of the Heart's Delight: Bruce McGill, Hiro Narita, Peter Postlethwaite

not know when was the right moment to start and how much until the editing was complete. The right moment came when a riotous crowd breaks into a jail at night to extricate the falsely accused man in total darkness except for the flash lights they carried. I used the flash lights as the source of illumination as they created frantic, nightmarish effects I did not quite foresee. Off camera, my gaffer carried a small battery-operated lamp simulating and augmenting the flashlights. The result was chaotic, frenzied, and impressionistic; unrehearsed cinematic moments which I must admit I truly loved. It is not an exaggeration to say that the scene was lit by the extras. And I could not have captured such images without the high-def digital camera. Also, in the climatic lynching scene at night in a park, I took advantage of onlookers' car headlights (some were replaced with our movie lights for intensity and durability) so we could freely look into them. I was very excited by the images we captured, beyond my own expectation. They were in a sense improvised and even accidental. I learned this tactic from my documentary shootings; keep my mind's eye open and see-san francisco

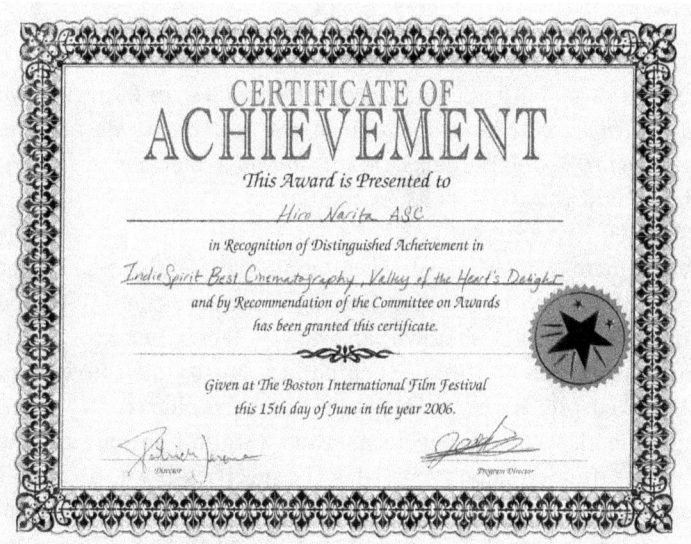

Certificate of Achievement, Boston International Film Festival

preconception put on hold for the moment–and discover whatever presents itself before the camera.

The English actor Pete Postlethwaite was nominated for an Oscar for In the Name of the Father (1993) *directed by Jim Sheridan. Steven Spielberg at the time of their collaboration in Amistad (1997), hailed him as "the best actor in the world". What do you remember about his interpretation?*

Postlethwaite (remarkable in *In the Name of the Father*) played a tycoon publisher. In this period drama he came across vividly as the man in pursuit of political power, manipulating and jury-rigging the evidence. He was excellent as always. Off camera, however, he was reclusive and I rarely saw him beyond the set. Ten years earlier I worked with him on *James and Giant Peach*, playing a mysterious story-teller, and I asked him if he remembered me, but he said no. He must have been totally preoccupied in his role.

hiro narita. depth of field

Shrink Rap *is a British television series hosted by clinical psychologist Dr. Pamela Stephenson in which she interviews various celebrities using psychotherapeutic techniques. In 2007 you collaborated as a camera operator on one of the episodes, the one with actor Robin Williams. What do you remember about Williams? Did you like him as an actor?*

A cinematographer friend asked me to operate a second camera for the Robin Williams interview. My camera was on Dr. Stephenson over Williams' shoulder, and he was facing her with several Rorschach tests on the wall behind her. During the conversation she asked him his responses on each of the charts. As you can imagine his extemporaneous answers were so hilarious and outrageous–though I don't remember the specifics–it was difficult to keep myself from bursting out in laughter. If I did, I hope the mic did not pick any of it. A great actor and performer he was, Williams was whimsical and boundless as a person.

In Generic Thriller (2009) *by Scott Sublett and* All About Dad (2009) *by Mark Tran, you worked as a visual consultant. What exactly does it consist of?*

These two projects were student films at San Jose State University, California, where I taught cinematography classes during two summer sessions. I supervised and consulted the student cinematographers and gaffers as if they were in an actual professional film production. And following a generic industry crew call-sheet, each student was assigned a job to fulfill. This was an effective course taught by an adjunct professor, also a professional assistant director/production manager in the industry.

How was your experience in La Mission, *directed by Peter Bratt, brother of Benjamin Bratt in 2009? The film is played by the same Benjamin Bratt, who plays Che Rivera growing up in the Mission District of San Francisco.*

san francisco

I felt very at home working on *La Mission*, the story based on the lives of Latino culture in a section of San Francisco. Director Peter Bratt, a Latino filmmaker himself, embodied his ethnic culture and had an insider's perspective of the people and their bearings. Bratt's brother Benjamin Bratt (*Law and Order*), playing the main role, also grew up in the city.
The Mission district is full of colorful murals and artifacts like an outdoor open art gallery. Fascinating and delightful to tourists, underneath the surface is a complex subculture, and I wanted to learn much from them as my knowledge was sketchy and superficial. Brad wanted to show familiar, photogenic spots in the film, but only incidentally in the background, as the fabric of the district. Vivid colors everywhere enthralled me and I wanted to capture them, yet refrained from showcasing them. The story dealt with a single father and his gay son who is ostracized by him. The father's face-saving dogma eventually get shattered by his close friends. For the film, it was proposed to make the image gritty, desaturated, and even grainy. I expressed to Bratt that it was not a true portrayal of the Mission district and its people. I was not persuaded by the trendy visual treatment of the time in TV commercials and movies. In my opinion, visual elements that adorned the streets were essential "characters" in the story and they needed to "speak." Bratt was happy to hear my thought. Juxtaposed with the main theme there was another element the Latinos commonly embraced: lowrider. We had them through the movie as a tangible connection between the estranged father and the son. When the filming of lowriders' gathering was publicly announced, double the number of cars we expected showed up under Bay Bridge that night. It was an extraordinary site to see over one hundred custom-built cars, adding to the flavor of the subculture.

Without border

2010s-2020s

Love & Taxes (2015) *is a riveting comedy tale of seven years of tax avoidance. Following the possibly real-life exploits of Josh Kornbluth, an autobiographical monologist. It is directed by Jacob Kornbluth, brother of Josh Kornbluth. What is there to say about this great mix of a theatrical monologue combined with dramatizations covering certain events in Josh's life?*

Josh Kornbluth is a unique and brilliant monologist on stage and a film actor. Based on his monologue, the film was a combination of his stage performance intertwined with a film re-enactment of the play. It was an inventive and amusing project filmed in San Francisco and New York locations. We built sets in a small studio on a shoestring budget and even used visual effects created by a freelance animator. With a small group of dedicated people, we shot it intermittently over a year as Kornbluth raised the production fund.

With Josh Kornbluth, you worked also in Strange culture (2007).

Kornbluth appeared as a college professor in *Strange Culture* directed by Lynn Hershman Leeson. He also appeared in *Teknolust* and *The Darwin's Award* as comedic characters.

What can you tell me about your last film Love Is Love Is Love *(2020), an American drama film directed by Eleanor Coppola, in which you photographed the segment* Late Lunch? *Late Lunch: a tragic loss brings together a disparate group (including Cybill Shepherd, Rosanna Arquette, and Rita Wilson) for a memorial meal hosted by their mutual friend's daughter (Maya Kazan, granddaughter of film director Elia Kazan). The title of the film combines the three stories (the other two are* Two For Dinner *and* Sailing Lesson*) that explore themes of love, commitment and loyalty within the couple and between friends.*

Late Lunch, is a triptych in *Love Is Love Is Love*, written and directed by Eleanor Coppola (*Paris Can Wait, Hearts of Darkness*): it's a drama but, as Coppola explained, with a flavor of documentary. In the story ten women sit at a long dining table one afternoon, reminiscing about a recently deceased friend. Filming for eight days in a San Francisco location posed logistic and technical hurdles; to maintain a consistent "one afternoon" look–visual uniformity was essential–while changing sunlight and varying weather complicated the lighting set-ups. My gaffer Eric Blum (*The Valley of the Hearts Delight, La Mission*) and I planned a manageable and flexible lighting scheme with small HMIs that can be powered by house electricity–a generator was not a solu-

Late Lunch: Hiro Narita with director Eleanor Coppola and producer Anahid Nazarian. Photo by Karman Muller (courtesy of American Zoetrope)

tion in the dense residential district–creating a consistent sunlight effect while blocking the ever-shifting real sun. For the interior, by minimizing lights on the floor, I wanted the actors to feel unrestrained. I wanted them to feel they are at a real lunch gathering. To maintain the interior ambience, we hung Kino Flo tubes with diffusions above the windows facing south and left them in the same position for the duration of the shoot. With the benefit of 4K digital photography, we were able to film under relatively low light conditions without sacrificing the quality.

What can you tell me about Eleanor as a director?

Eleanor Coppola is a very accomplished director in both narrative and documentary genres; she is also a talented cinematographer and artist who collaborated with Lynn Hershman Leeson (*Teknolust*) in the 70s and their friendship still continues. *Late Lunch*, she reminded me often, should be enveloped in the spirit of a real atmosphere. I strove to maintain the atmosphere, and wide shots and details create visual and emotional rhythm, providing the editor with enough images to build that rhythm in editing. In a larger context, the camera should become an unobtrusive participant in the lunch as well as an observer of the event.

How did you plan your work?

During pre-production, as I planned the filming strategy with Coppola, I felt strongly a need for another eye on the set, not only to meet the daily schedule, but to add a visual perspective of another cinematographer. I asked camera person Dyanna Taylor, an experienced director and cinemaphotographer of many documentary films. In some respects, I was looking for less contrived images from the B camera. With each scene-blocking, we would determine the "A" camera position first in a conscious way, and give the "B" camera a liberal rein of camera angles. And whenever the space allowed, we used camera sliders to facilitate adjustment to the composition while the cameras were rolling, adding a sense of spontaneity. In a movie, reality and fiction intersect, or else the boundary becomes indistinct in our mind. *Late Lunch* was such a movie.

What model of camera did you shoot with?

I used two Sony FS7 in 4K owned by Zoetrope, which Francis Coppola used to film his last three films. I understand that the camera was developed or modified by Sony following Coppola's recommendation. To the camera package I added few zoom lenses and 180mm lens for *Late Lunch*.

Late Lunch *also stars Cybill Shepherd, interpreter of New Hollywood films such as* The Last Picture Show *(1971) by Peter Bogdanovich and* Taxi Driver *(1976) by Martin Scorsese. What do you remember Cybill Shepherd? How did you work together?*

Had I not known it was Cybill Shepherd from the celebrated movies, I would have thought she was another actress playing a role in the film. Much to our delight and making our work easier,

Late Lunch: Hiro Narita with director Eleanor Coppola.
Photo by Karman Muller (courtesy of American Zoetrope)

she was casual on and off the set, and memorably, she kept us chuckling with her dry humor all through the production. For eight days of filming, except during the camera angle changes, the actors remained at the table. Because they were not told who the B camera was filming, they all stayed in character.

The New Hollywood, also referred to as the American New Wave refers to a movement in American film history from the mid-1960s to the early 1980s. What do you remember about The New Hollywood years?

It was an exciting time in the US cinema when many young filmmakers were impacted by the French New Wave, by its principles. John Cassavetes and Arthur Penn among the forerunners to embrace the movement, a creative new energy surged through young directors. They also took notice of Japanese films that were riding their own waves around the same time.
I can speak about my recollection of the period only in thumbnail sketches. Directors like François Truffaut, who loved and admired the old Hollywood films, rejected traditional filmmaking to find their own way, their niche, along with his contemporaries. Still concerned with troubling social and political affairs in Europe, they channeled their ideas into innovative and experimental filmmaking without the heavy production mechanism on their shoulders. I think the time was ripe for the New Wave to reach US shores, and a renaissance was inevitable in US cinema. Moving from the Midwest, John Korty had already established his grounds in Stinson Beach in 1964 and was making films independently. Inspired by Korty and thinking this was what they had dreamed of, Coppola, Lucas, Ballard, and others, made a courageous, daring move to San Francisco, creating American Zoetrope and establishing their new base away from Hollywood, joining the ranks of progressive filmmakers Scorsese and Mazursky alike in New York. In response to the significant movement, remodeling got under way in the old Hollywood structure itself, and I was fortunate to see it all happen before my eyes.

Hiro Narita (from behind), actress Joan Chen and director Lynn Hershman Leeson (from behind) on the movie set *Logic Paralyzes the Heart* (2022). Photo by Pamela Gentile

Director Lynn Hershman Leeson (sitting), Hiro Narita and gaffer Eric Blum on the set of *Logic Paralyzes the Heart*, (2022) Photo Pamela Gentile

hiro narita. depth of field

What project have you been working on lately?

In 2021 I participated in Lynn Hershman Leeson's latest short film *Logic Paralyzes the Heart*, her ongoing investigation into cyborg and its effect on the human mind and behavior. Against a green screen we filmed Joan Chen (*The Last Emperor*). She played both the cyborg and the narrator who interviews her. Being nearly identical in both characters, dressed in the same costume, she gave an uncanny sense of two worlds mirroring each other. Hershman Leeson then integrated them into other images and graphics of current relevance. As with Tilda Swinton, Chen, now a longtime resident of San Francisco, was aware of the evolution of the human and cybernetic synthesis and she was excited to be part of the project. The film will be shown at the 59th Biennale in Venice.

Considerations on the cinema and beyond

Which film of the past impressed you most in terms of cinematography in your artistic training?

Certain movies left a strong impression on me, and as time passed, other great movies impacted me also; all stacked on top of each other in my memory. It is difficult to single out which movie inspired me the most. I drew countless lessons from films all over the world and have come to believe there are no boundaries in the geography of the mind, as Takemitsu said of Noguchi's travel. All things said and considered, however partial, I would choose the cinematography in *The Last Emperor* by Vittorio Storaro as the most inspiring film in my mid-career. In a way, it was a textbook for cinematography and I used it later in my film classes. His aesthetic lighting and the use of bleach bypass processing in some parts of the film embraced realism and fantasy in historical scope and emotional validity. In the interior of the Empress's palace, just as an example, the shaft of sunlight poured only through selected windows. But to our eyes, it was heightened reality, not realism in the conventional sense. Storaro's exploration into light and color in moving images awakened me: it was what painters centuries ago practiced and achieved on canvas. The film stirred me toward a new visual horizon, corroborating the notion that imagination so often overrides logic.
There is an early Kurosawa film *Stray Dog* (1949, black and white). I saw it probably in the late 1970 and I was struck by the heat and humidity playing a major role in the story of a young detective, whose gun was stolen from him and a murder committed with it. Shimmering sweat and sluggishness caused by the swelter-

ing weather was so much a part of the characters' dialogues, feelings and actions. Besides the atmosphere, there were many interesting compositions, distinctive of many of Kurosawa's later films, consisting of separate actions occupying the upper and lower frame, or background action drawing just as much attention as the foreground; and the economy of expressing complex ideas in a single frame. *Stray Dog* is a seminal work in Kurosawa's illustrious career.

To the list I would add *How Green Was My Valley* (1941) by John Ford, photographed by Arthur C. Miller (another black & white film). It struck me how each frame was not only beautifully composed and lit but also said so much. I thought the cinematography embraced Italian neo-realism and impressionism in art. An interesting anecdote–for a film historian–is that Ford exposed just enough film to make the final edit, so that producer Darryl Zanuck had no way of changing it; Ford exercised his ultimate control. Also, the fact that the mining town in Wales was entirely built and filmed on Santa Cruz mountain in southern California was itself an incredible accomplishment.

What were your most favourite or memorable scenes to light, and can you describe the process and how you did the lighting for the scenes?

In *The Rocketeer* there were many light changes during the dance sequence in the South Sea Club. Thanks to computer-assisted dimmer boards, I could repeat the light changes synchronized with the pre-recorded music. Importantly, I wanted the viewer not to be distracted by them as an effect, but be absorbed in the emotional continuity of the scene. As the actors danced, I wanted them to look beautiful under the seductive lights or look seductive under the deceptive lights. Sometimes it takes a complex technique to achieve a simple, seemingly effortless image. From what I remember in Fellini's *8 ½*, the emotional continuity and the visual continuity are two sides of a coin. *The Rocketeer* was technically very complex, yet the result looked effortless.

considerations on the cinema and beyond

I am also proud of the images from the jail and the lynching scenes in *Valley of The Heart's Delight* in which the lighting was essentially improvised and realism intensified. Of course, a few adjustments were made for certain camera angles during filming. The sensitivity of the digital camera made it possible to capture those extemporaneous moments. And importantly, my documentary experiences taught me not to let the flashes of beautiful moments slip by my very eyes.
Through the years there have been moments of great satisfaction and disappointment in my own work. Looking back, putting my thought to evaluating my capacity or limitations, I cherish the opportunities I had of filming many captivating stories and events in different lights.

Which Italian cinematographers, past and present, do you most admire?

There are many extraordinary cinematographers in Italy, past and present. Some of them have made great contributions to American movies and inspired students of cinematography. Giuseppe Rotunno and Vittorio Storaro come to my mind immediately. Storaro's understanding of light and color expanded the visual language of cinema, bridging what is seen and what is felt, and reaching straight to our emotions. Fellini's *8 1/2*, photographed by Gianni Di Venanzo, opened my eyes. The camera is active; it moves along with actors or weaves through scenes. The camera seems like another character in the scene or an inquisitive spectator. There were lighting changes in the middle of a scene or camera movements that produced unique sensations: they were more than just eye-catching or sweeping tracking shots. They were, I believe, amorphous sensations that aroused and gave life to the viewing experience.

New technology: what do you think of the epochal transition from film to digital?

Many avid dialogues and debates on the subject have arisen and been exchanged. In my lifetime, we have gone from black-and-white, color negative and reversal, magnetic, and now to digital medium. Cinema, a synthesis of art and technology, evolved from silent movies to talkies–a far greater leap in technique and process than today's shift from film grains to digital pixels. We should not confuse the limitations and potentials of different media with our own blindness or limited vision. I see so much potential in the digital tool, opening the door to an expanded spectrum of color, for instance, which until now, has been veiled under our conditioned or biased perception. I hope the new technology will help merge our visual and emotional experience. I dived into the new technology over twenty years ago and have never looked back.

How could you describe your cinematography style?

I'd like to say I have an "approach" to my work, not necessarily a "style". A director has his vision or visual concept, and a cinematographer's role is a collaborative one, to achieve and enhance the director's vision. In doing so, the cinematographer's personal perception and understanding of light, shadow, and color inevitably seep out, becoming a form of personal expression. But it is shaped by his understanding of the story presented before him. Ultimately, the story dictates visual style, I believe. Art direction, editing, and a myriad of day-to-day production complexities and limitations under the director's control contribute to the final outcome. We all make preconceived assessments, but I take them as a starting point, allowing discovery to navigate. In that sense, I do have my approach. I am sometimes praised and sometimes accused of my chameleon-like work: so many styles. Some cinematographers are said to impose their style on the films they shoot. But I think their so-called style is a result of life experience, mature recognition of both empirical reality and their mind's eye.

considerations on the cinema and beyond

You are a member of the ASC-American Society of Cinematographers - the oldest continuously operating motion picture society in the world - since 1993: which ASC cinematographers recommended you for membership?

Haskell Wexler, Stephen H. Burum, and Robert Primes wrote me letters of recommendation for ASC membership.

How has ASC membership impacted your life and career?

It is a great honor to be included in the ASC, a very respected society in the movie industry and membership represents one's qualification and professionalism; but importantly, the society promotes the art of cinematography and through its various members shares unique talent around the world. I am honored to be part of it.

You are also a member of the Academy Motion Picture Arts and Sciences. *In what year did you join it? Regarding the nominations, can you only vote for your category (Best Cinematography)? In choosing the winners of the Oscars, can every member of the Academy vote for each category?*

I was invited to join the Academy in 1992 just after the release of *Star Trek VI*. As for Oscar voting, the Academy sends out the list of national and international films that are qualified under its rule; usually there are three to four hundred films each year. Initially we submit our nomination only in our own category; in my case, Best Cinematography. After the Academy has tabulated the ballots and announced the nominees in all categories, we then cast our final vote. But we need not vote, say, for the best song or the best animation, if we do not feel confident in making the decision.

You have earned comparison with the legendary James Wong Howe ASC who won two Academy Awards for The Rose Tattoo

hiro narita. depth of field

(1955) and Hud *(1963). Both of you have managed to establish yourself in American cinema, coming from another continent, Asia, obviously at different times, Howe started working right from silent movie ... When you were taking your first steps in the film industry, did you know Howe's work?*

I have not heard of comparison with James Wong How, and it is an honor I absolutely do not deserve. When he entered the movie industry, technology was still archaic and new photographic techniques were being experimented. In this climate, Wong How was very innovative in his craft and, importantly, progressive in his art; he was a trailblazer as a cinematographer. Above and beyond, he overcame the social environment that was unfavorable to Asian Americans, managing to jump over the hurdles steadfastly and remaining creative. With my generation I can say I was a beneficiary of his deeds without the burden he carried on his shoulder. *The Rose Tattoo*–magnificent in many ways–and *The Molly Maguires* are examples of his work I like very much.

I guess you haven't had a chance to meet him, talk to him personally because Howe died in 1976?

A special tribute to James Wong How was held by the San Francisco International Film Festival not long before his death; my wife and I attended the event and saw him on stage answering questions from the audience. I was nailed to the seat absorbing his glowing face. With such a frail body, assisted by his wife, he retraced his career as if remembering dreams. In awe, I watched this legendary man recounting the long road he trod.

The Italian cinematographers Luciano Tovoli and Vittorio Storaro, members of AIC and ASC, were among the major animators of the battle for the recognition of copyright for cinematographers. What do you think of the concept of authorship for your category?

I have experienced my work looking different on release from what I signed off at the end of the final color grading. This is a major issue to fight for as cinematographers, and it must be resolved. Allen Daviau fought for the authorship of cinematography and led this important movement tirelessly. Especially in the digital world, engineers have so much control with the touch of dials and affect the end result. Cinematography is a personal expression, a personal art, and without the author's consent, his work should not be altered.

Over the course of your career, which camera model did you prefer?

Panavision, Arriflex, and Aaton were the cameras I used for film, and Sony and Canon for digital cinematography, sometimes by choice, often owing to the producers' budgetary reasons. I paid special attention to the choice of lenses, regardless of which camera body I used.

Have you worked in commercials? If so, can you tell me for which brands and what are the main differences you encountered from working on a film?

In my mid-career I shot commercials for several years. In fact, I worked with one local director exclusively for promoting San Francisco Giants baseball team and Napa County tourism–with no products to sell directly–mainly humorous ones he was well known for. In the late 90s a cosmetic company in Japan asked me to shoot a commercial with Pierce Brosnan after he became the latest James Bond. The director came from Japan, but the filming was organized by an American company and we filmed it in a desert east of Los Angeles. Brosnan as a Bond-like character drove a sports car and at the end mentioned the product, clean and simple. I filmed him again the following year for the same company, in a different environment. While waiting between set-ups, Brosnan drew sketches in pen-and-ink. The ones he showed me were

hiro narita. depth of field

very intricate, almost surrealistic, images of flora and fauna. He said it was his love after acting. Commercials are amusing in the sense that you have to promote and sell an idea or a product in 60 seconds or less. They are different from long format film; yet there are many lessons to be learned from them.

About the James Bond saga, what do you think of the secret agent created by the British journalist and novelist Ian Fleming? Are you passionate about these movies or not?

I admit I have seen only bits and pieces of Bond films since Sean Connery's early versions, except the latest, *No Time to Die*, which I thought was visually stunning and beautifully made. I cannot dismiss the value of such thrillers for entertainment, but I never kept up with 007 or with most of the action movies.

Is there an anecdote about your career you want to remember?

It sounds naïve but I did not realize cinematographers can be typecast like actors. After *Never Cry Wolf* was released, the films offered to me dealt with animals: a girl with a horse, a boy with

Actor Pierce Brosnan and Hiro Narita on a Japanese commercial

considerations on the cinema and beyond

a wolf, etc. I was labeled a specialist in visual effects-laden projects at another point. I am glad that I was involved in a variety of genres, adding more apparatus to my tool box and addressing the evolving technology in filmmaking. I can see now the common term; you are as good as your last picture. I mulled over my career and then took a conscious step to work on smaller, independent films in the San Francisco area, not so much an attempt to avoid being typecast, but I felt at home dealing with stories about the people in the area I knew.

What was your crew, your most loyal collaborators?

I have worked with many skilled and devoted crews over the years. When it comes to selecting my crew, I first pick my assistant cameraman. It is very important to me because this individual must be technically proficient and, at the same time, he remains almost invisible to the actors in front of the camera and creates an amicable atmosphere around the camera. The combination is not easily found. Then I select a gaffer or chief lighting man with whom I can communicate well enough to use simple sign language. Luckily, I worked with the same crew almost always in Hollywood, eliminating superfluous talk on the set. In the San Francisco area too, I had a similar group of people working together with me. On distant locations though, I was obliged to use the local crew; not a perfect situation sometimes. But I found many talented people in unexpected places.

Which actors and actresses you have worked with have impressed you the most?

Tilda Swinton comes to my mind first. She was a true collaborator beyond being an actress. Having worked with Derek Jarman in her early career, an association which rooted in her the notion of the artistic community, the company, she made us feel equal partners in the process. In each role she played she embodied the character, setting aside her own self. Yet when the camera stopped rolling, in nanoseconds, she was back to the Swinton we can have conversation and share tea or coffee with. When we were preparing *Teknolust*, the makeup artist experimented three distinct looks on each of Rosetta Stone's (Swinton's) clones. Heavily made up, Swinton reacted to how she looked in the mirror and said, I could play three different clones without making me visibly different, just give me different wigs. She was absolutely right. Not only could she play three clone characters plus Rosetta Stone with nuance and subtlety, they were all interesting, and she saved so much production time.

Which director you worked with was the most attentive and interested in cinematography?

Without a doubt, Carroll Ballard is the most experienced, and he was genuinely interested in cinematography; esthetically and technically. His documentary *Harvest* (nominated for Oscar in 1968 for best documentary) already showed his uncompromising tenacity in finding images not just for their beauty but for their essence. He owned several Aaton CM3 cameras and a large collection of lenses, just as a craftsman owns his tools, the extension of his hands and his eyes. When Ballard explained a scene to me, he used his hands and wild gestures, never specifically pictorial, but they translated into images vividly and more clearly in my mind.

Is there a director you would have liked to collaborate with?

Thoughts occurred to me in the past, wishing I could have been involved in certain films. There are many directors whose work I appreciate and love, yet, I have not actively entertained nor pursued the idea of working with particular directors because of their work. But when I saw films like *Il postino* (director: Michael Redford) and *The King's Speech* (director, Tom Hooper), for instance, I wish I had been part of the projects. Both films, while they are different in content and visual parameter, impacted me viscerally; that is, the contextual voice and visual complimented and supported each other, revealing strata of experiences I can connect. I suppose I could have persuaded my agent in Hollywood to send my resume to these directors I was interested in, but I never did.

Have you had friends among your colleagues? Is there any one that you admired?

There are many colleagues whose work I admire immensely. But I knew very few personally. Caleb Deschanel, Haskell Wexler, and Stephen Goldblatt are among those I came to know. I think Goldblatt's work display his boundless inventiveness: his shoot-from-the-hip instinct needed to capture "the moment" and then shift to stylized and studied images with ease and eloquence. Interestingly, they all have their beginnings in documentary films. The ASC club house provides a perfect place to socialize with colleagues, and through various seminars it holds you can meet your contemporaries and retirees or future members. Regrettably, I have attended just a few of them since I live far away from Hollywood.

From the auditions of The Godfather *to* Apocalypse Now *to conclude with* Love Is Love Is Love: *both you and your wife Barbara have been linked to the Coppola family. What can you tell me further, have there also been occasions for meetings outside work?*

Thinking back, it is interesting to realize that my life has crisscrossed with the Coppolas several times over the last fifty years. Working at American Zoetrope in the early 70s, I first became friends with Eleanor's brother Bill Neil (*The Fifth Element, Superman Returns*), who was installing an advanced sound system in the studio where I met my future wife. Bill assisted me as assistant cameraman on my first feature *Silence* and he went on to become an accomplished visual effects director of photography and a member of ASC. I did not know Eleanor well, but she was often mentioned in my conversation with Lynn Hershman Leeson, and Eleanor was part of the visual history of artists Hershman Leeson has been compiling through her career and I filmed her interview. She also worked on *Teknolust* as additional camera operator. In recent years I met Francis, after nearly fifty years, when I went to see Eleanor for the preproduction meeting in his studio, also at Bill's 80th birthday lunch held at Coppola's winery. I am truly appreciative of the fact that the film community in northern California, small but prominent, has intertwined in inexplicable ways, shaping our lives (my wife's and mine) and our careers; a realization I marvel at and treasure today. One brief episode: In 1990 Akira Kurosawa came to Hollywood to receive the Academy's Lifetime Achievement Award and Coppola brought him to his house in San Francisco. My wife and I were kindly invited on this occasion and we met Kurosawa. It was a reverential and courtesy greeting on my part, but what a thrilling moment! It is deeply etched into my heart.

You were interviewed by your colleague John Fauer ASC, director of the documentary Cinematographer Style *(2006). Fauer pays homage to the artists who transform ideas into images, interviewing 110 leading cinematographers from around the world, including you. What do you remember of that experience? On that occasion you were included among the most important cinematographers in the world like Vittorio Storaro, Gordon Willis, Haskell Wexler, Vilmos Zsigmond, Owen Roizman...*

Fauer (publisher, Film and Digital Times) interviewed me once for his magazine, and later for this documentary. At the time I was aware to some degree of the value of his documentary, visual records in an oral history of cinematographers. I was honored to take part. Then I realized it was an important, if not ambitious, project documenting the path we cinematographers took and the principles behind our work. Supported by Arri, Kodak, and Technicolor in addition to many colleagues in the field, the documentary is a valuable visual record of the people who contributed to the art of cinematography.

considerations on the cinema and beyond

You taught at the San Francisco Art Institute: what have you tried to convey to your students?

For eight years I taught cinematography at San Francisco Art Institute, my alma mater, making a full circle in my career. It was a time of personal reflection, and a time of sharing my experiences with students who were not necessarily film majors but interested in another form of visual expression. Meshing together moving images of different scale and rhythm challenged their unexplored territory of art form. Whether in narrative or experimental format, filmmaking enabled them to delve into what was unexplored in their minds. I recognized their eccentric and, at times, idiosyncratic attempts at making a film, but I witnessed their pure and direct voices.

Creativity happens randomly; it is a result of many ideas and thoughts–even daydreams–colliding and coalescing, eventually making themselves manifest. A film is a complex but ultimately an ideal tool of personal expression, I told my students and myself. Cinematography is inexplicably related to painting, music, and even acting; creating emotional cadence and mood beyond images. For students, studying technical lighting should be ancillary to seeing and discovering images that communicate deep emotions. Lighting, so called "painting with light" is a very personal art, and it sometimes involves cutting the light off. I often borrow the phrase from Japanese cinema, "the beauty of things you don't see". What is unlit in the corner, what is off screen beyond the frame line, are also part of the viewing experience, sometimes one that is more powerful than what is fully seen. For me there is a continual interplay in filmic storytelling between what is manifested on the screen and what is suggested.

As students develop "seeing", lighting becomes a necessary tool to enhance whatever is presented before the camera. The light illuminates allegorical information in a view that words do not fully convey.

If you look at movies from the thirties and forties, you will find many masterful examples of this. They knew how to bring a story to an audience and bring an audience into a story. Studying examples of masterful cinematography, you see the lighting in itself seems to lack or even violate logic; light transmits emotions and sensations which the observer translates or decodes into personal experience. I believe discovering what light does and, what people see in it is more important than learning the conventional key-light, back-light, fill-light concept or other formulas.

I really like the phrase you just quoted "the beauty of things you don't see." Have you picked it up from Japanese cinema, from any film in particular?

Actually, a Japanese commercial director told me the phrase when we were discussing the composition and the lighting of a shot. I asked him if he wanted to see an object behind the actor. He said, keep it in the dark, just a suggestion is more interesting. Then he used the phrase, "the beauty of things you don't see," which he said is an important notion in Japanese cinema. Derived, I believe, from historical handscroll paintings or woodblock prints, even "haiku" poems, it has been a highly developed artform in Japan for centuries; intentionally truncating or omitting things, not only for the sake of economy, but to allow the missing parts to be filled in by the viewer's imagination, his spirit of inquiry. In a sense, there is no empty space in a frame; it is all part of the active viewing experience, and besides, the interplay of what is seen and not seen is very dynamic. Along this line of thinking, the back of an actor at a certain moment is as revealing as his face and the viewer's mental picture of him is potent. I saw such instances in many Japanese movies, old and new.

You have also taught master classes at many institutions including Golden Eye in the Republic of Georgia.

The San Francisco Film Society (the organizer of the San Francisco International Film Festival) has a variety of programs to educate and inspire young filmmakers; in writing, directing, and

considerations on the cinema and beyond

in other crafts taught by professionals in their fields. I gave a lighting class several times in the program, as well as in other groups that organized such events.

The Golden Eye International Festival of Cameramen was held in the Republic of Georgia; the home base of Sergei Parajanof (*Shadow of Forgotten Ancestors*). His films inspired me years ago. I did not know how they found me in such a faraway country, but I was thrilled to attend. My wife was also excited and urged me to go because she was there in 1986 via the Soviet Union touring with the Women in Film of San Francisco. There she met women directors and invited them to showcase their films in San Francisco. Besides judging cinematography in different categories such as narrative, documentary, and journalistic report during the festival, I presented my brief view of cinematographic styles in movies and my own sample work.

Georgia, nestled on the corner of the Black Sea, with Russia to the north and surrounded by Turkey, Azerbaijan, and Armenia, was once part of the Silk Road, a channel between East and West. The mosaic of rich by-gone cultures still remains; and it is no mystery to find that cinema has flourished and the country has produced many memorable films seen throughout the world. I felt a familiarity in Georgia that I could not clearly define. Even though my ear was hearing Georgian, Russian, English, and a multitude of languages from the Caucasus, I truly felt that cinema cut through cultural boundaries and spoke one language. During the several trips I made to Georgia in subsequent years I met Lana Gogoberidze (*Day is Longer Than Night*) whom my wife met in Georgia. And an unforgettable event took place at the end of the festival when the son of Sofiko Chiaureli, the legendary actress in several of Parajanov's films, gave each juror a beautiful picture book on his mother's life and career. His gesture brought me even closer to Georgian filmmakers.

From Georgia to the Eurasian International Film Festival in Kazakhstan in 2016 and 2018.

hiro narita. depth of field

The Georgian connection led me to the Eurasian International Film Festival in Kazakhstan in 2016 and 2018. In Kazakhstan, the classes were more like a seminar for film students and anyone interested in such an event. I was invited to the film department in an incredibly modern art school (a national institution) for a Q&A session with the students. The camera department head showed me their latest camera acquisition (4K Arri-Alexa) and mentioned that the students must first learn about the camera inside out, including its repair; only then are they allowed to photograph. I responded by saying, I am a cinematographer and I think of the images in front of the camera first, and honestly, I am technically inept. He had a big smile on his face and whispered to me, "We still teach the old Soviet method." I understood that there are different routes to reach the same goal.

The enduring impacts from Soviet cinema were evident in the early history of Kazakh films. But now they are finding their own voice. Through new technology, global communication is nearly instantaneous, and sharing movies worldwide has become routine. At the end the festival, the chair of the jurors Vladimir

Hiro Narita and Sergei Parajanof statue in Tbilisi

considerations on the cinema and beyond

Eurasia International Film Festival, Narita's seminar announcement, Kazakhstan (2018)

Menshov (*Moscow Dose Not Believe in Tears*) from Russia addressed, literally implored, the young filmmakers in the audience, "Do not imitate others, have faith in your own culture and the uniqueness of who you are." Understandably, he was witnessing films indistinguishable from one another–from China, from Russia, or from the USA–and the abundance of technical skill and extravaganza was overshadowing the content. Reliance on digital technology is a global phenomenon. On the other hand, there are many positive sides to it; the ability to put on screen what has only been in our imagination.

We aspire to be creative pioneers, catalysts, and in doing so, we plow our own field. I agreed with Menshov that we should not be tempted to take short cuts and simply emulate others, ignoring our own thoughts and feelings; he meant that the new tool is readily available not just in the hands of a select few. Let's use it with honest and genuine sense. I felt as if I had met another teacher halfway around the world, yet he seemed like a next door-neighbor.

What is your relationship with young filmmakers?

In recent years I have been participating in judging domestic and international narrative short films for the Student Academy Awards. They represent a broad range of subjects; some dealing with global issues, and others examining personal exploits. I believe that young filmmakers are at a juncture where the new tools enable them to explore and enrich their cinematic expressions. Technology has made a big leap, as we experienced from the silent to talking movies in the past and now from film to the digital domain, and our mind should not lag behind it. Our complex mind has yet to be fully realized in cinema, and I have great hopes of seeing young filmmakers breathe new life into it.

How has cinema changed since your beginnings? Is the film industry today different from the way films were made when you trained and worked?

Technology has unleashed so much creative potential that filmmakers could not have imagined it just a decade ago. But I see some narrative films curiously overlapping with animations, or vice versa, in their imageries. This is not a negative observation, but I hope the trend will not fall into creating restless, short bursts of images, however sensational they may be, designed for small screens confined in a living room. Is it inevitable? A noticeable change has taken place in the film industry structure in recent years; the old studio systems have shifted toward corporate business ventures and the film outlet no longer depends on movie theaters. This I believe may have a bigger and lasting impact on filmmaking.

considerations on the cinema and beyond

In more direct and immediate ways, to our advantage as cinematographers, we now take control of what the camera captures right on the spot. And the lab, so to speak, is always at out fingertips, instead of being in a building in another city miles away. This takes an enormous load off us and eliminates one big step; the initial stage of color grading. And in postproduction we can make selective–within a frame–adjustments, equivalent to a painter touching up a picture on canvas; an unthinkable feat in the past. And for editors, in spite of having to deal with far more elaborate equipment than ever before, their greater ability to create alternate edits and preserve them instantly is an incredible breakthrough.

Our affinity to tell stories, hear them or see them in visual forms is as old as the dawn of history and I hope we carry forward this heritage, expanding with the help of new technologies.

What's the best professional advice you've ever received?

I must go back to my design class in school. The instructor told us to draw a cat as best we could. He then asked, "Are you happy with it? If you are, please throw it away and draw another best one from a different angle." A few drawings later he explained that our first attempt was from our memory and we must not be attached to what you think is the best or the most precious at that moment. Do not put a price tag on your work; do not measure your worth. That exercise taught me and has stayed with me till this day. The lesson: A world opens its door when you shed your ego.

In your free time, do you have a particular passion, an interest outside cinema?

I have always liked tinkering with wood since my childhood. When I first married, I build a dining table–I still use it after 50 years–and set up a modest workshop in the basement. Ever since, my love of woodworking has broadened considerably, more than just a hobby, and I think sometimes I would be a cabinet maker if

Hiro Narita's woodwork

I had to choose my profession anew. Like sculpture, the esthetic and conceptual ideas in woodwork are expressed in three-dimensional, tangible objects. And unlike linear narrative storytelling or cinematography, a piece of woodwork encapsulates the arch of time all at once, and its story is self-contained. That is what attracts me very much. Besides, the scale of woodwork I engage in is measured against human dimensions and accessibility; concrete and practical. I also appreciate that each type of wood has its unique characteristics: grain pattern, color, and density, providing me with visual elements in advance. Working with wood demands craftsmanship and discipline; I am accountable only to myself and it is a thoroughly liberating experience. Since I am self-taught, I start with loose sketches and rough measurements and plunge right into cutting the wood, making alterations as I build; not really a proper or suitable method, and I catch myself failing to attend to the necessary structural requirements or taking into account the wood's shrinking and expanding behavior. On one project, to remedy my flaw, I decided to build a mock-up of a wooden table lamp comprising two tetrahedrons stacked together like an hour-glass. I had to ensure the dimensions and angles were correct and visually pleasing before I cut a single piece of wood. I spent a few months on the work but the result was fulfilling. Since moving to Petaluma thirty years ago, I have a large woodwork studio (20 feet x 80 feet) converted from an old chicken barn.

You told me about the company you started with your wife Barbara, called Pictures and Words. *Unfortunately, she passed away in 2013. Were you very united in your work too? You were her eyes and she your voice?*

My wife and I worked together for many years through our company Pictures & Words, but we also worked on projects for others directors. Her strength was in organizational skill and in her writing, an ideal combination as script supervisor and production manager. When I wrote articles for magazines, she would

Hiro Narita's woodwork

considerations on the cinema and beyond

Hiro Narita with his wife Barbara Parker Narita

check them and question me about what exactly I was trying to say in certain phrases. Inevitably, for lack of appropriate words, I would explain to her using images and jumbled words. She then interpreted them into proper phrases and idioms, organizing and clarifying my images/thoughts. In college, she told me, she studied architecture but eventually earned her Bachelor's degree in Anthropological Linguistics; a very esoteric study of language in which she recognized different cultures articulate and express their thoughts in particular ways; many seem strange because their perspective and emphasis differ from the Western thinking process. At one point in our marriage, to further her linguistic grasp, she attended the Monterey Defense Language Institute and took an intensive class in Japanese. During the period, the students lodged together in a dormitory for a month and they were not allowed to speak a word of English. I regret not asking her what motivated her to steer her career toward filmmaking after

hiro narita. depth of field

all the study she did. In her later life, after we closed our company, she volunteered for the local library selling surplus books to the public. Her joy in dealing with books was undeniable, physically handling, cataloging and displaying them for sale. I joined her sometimes for book sales and built a few display cases and an office desk in the library bookstore.

Hiro Narita in Rome 1986

considerations on the cinema and beyond

What did her parents do? Did they also work in the film industry or not?

Both Barbara's parents were gone before we were married. Her father was an aeronautical engineer who helped develop the passenger air control system for Douglas Aircraft Company, and her mother a jazz pianist who later worked for UNESCO; quite a family background she had.

Have you had any children?

We have no children of our own. But we helped our niece who became a fine still photographer, and now I am giving a helping hand to my nephew who is also leaning toward photography. For now, he is a computer expert and I call on his assistance whenever I have problems or need instructions.

You told me you shot twice in Luxembourg: were there any other European countries where you shot films?

Before I shot two films in Luxembourg, I took industrial stills in Austria, Belgium, France, Germany, Italy, and Norway; mostly underground telephone cables which utilized American heat shrinkable rubber sleeves. They were unusual assignments; I used to boast, jokingly, of my expertise in the underground of Europe.

Would you have liked to shot a movie in Italy?

Definitely, I wish I had had an opportunity to film in Italy, the country that has made so many contributions to the world of cinema. A long time ago during a photo shoot in Rome, I met a priest–I think he was just a friend of the American designer in charge of the photo session–who told me in length his analysis of Fellini and Antonioni. In his clerical collar he was a passionate film scholar in his own right and cinema was driven into his heart just as God was in his priesthood. I thought, this is Italy for you!

hiro narita. depth of field

In the United States, have you always lived in California, in the San Francisco area?

I left Hawaii in 1960 and moved to San Francisco city. Since then, with the exception of two years in the Army, I have always lived in the area; mostly to the north of the Golden Gate Bridge, known as Marin County and Sonoma County. Situated along the Pacific Ocean, the mild seasonal changes make the area very comfortable to live in.

Is it true that San Francisco is the most European city in the USA?

The city is the most cosmopolitan of all the places I have visited in the US. You may call it the most European in the sense that the architectural integrity and the variety of food available mirror the Old World. Italian restaurants are everywhere, so are Victorian houses. Europeans feel at home as they walk around and enjoy the city surrounded by the sea as if in the Mediterranean.

You have lived between South Korea, Japan and the United States. How did these different countries and cultures shape your personality?

It has been a long journey. I was four years old when we left Korea for Japan and I did not know Korea was a foreign country. While growing up I learned about Japanese atrocities and mistreatment of Koreans in their country and in Japan, and that the Japanese regarded Koreans as their inferiors. Since I was born there, I feared I would be mistaken by my friends as a Korean in their eyes. This childish complex and worry hung around my neck till I left Japan. When I lived in Hawaii and then in California–in multi-cultural environments–my view of people reshaped, and I told myself never to be one who belittles others. Gradually I learned to be empathetic and fair towards people who lived under racial prejudices, myself included. I have been very fortunate through my profession to have traveled to all fifty states in this country and to many others on the other side of the Atlantic Ocean. I witnessed the diversity of rich cultures and the people who inherit them and carry them forward. Especially, I found the world of art open and borderless unlike any other, allowing creative expression as the only mutual language to talk with one another from the heart, wherever you are and whoever you are. I found my home in it.

Which is the place you filmed that most impressed you?

Alaska and the Arctic circle gave me a life-changing, soul-stirring experience during the filming of *Never Cry Wolf*. Simply, the unimaginable vastness and the scale of nature made my presence so small and fragile like an ant in endless space. Yet the ant, against all odds, lived and had a role to play in it. It marked a shift in my perspective of life. I was a small piece in a jigsaw puzzle that makes up a large picture. I too had a role to play. The climate, which at times we complained of, not being in our favor, was in accord with the natural law of its own. I may sound as though I've dressed up my feelings, but living with these phenomena reshaped my frame of mind and gave me solace. As we completed the project, we landed first in Seattle, Washington, a beautiful and relatively unspoiled city. Yet I was overwhelmed by the noise, smell, and most of all, bewildered by how contrived the people looked; women in makeup and men with neckties, like beings from another world. Hesitantly, I had to readjust myself to so-called civilization. And it gave me a moment to reflect on what I had undergone in the north.
I rediscovered this quote by William Blake that expressed my sentiment at the time:

To see a World in a grain of Sand
And a Heaven in a Wild Flower.
Hold Infinity in the palm of your hand
And Eternity in an hour.

Testimonials

Lucille Carra

What more can be said about Hiro Narita, one of the best cinematographers of the last fifty years? His career has been varied and thrilling - he's been involved with some of the most iconic scenes in American film. He's filmed documentaries, blockbusters, concert films, and very notable television movies which elevated the art of cinematography on the small screen. Hiro started in the 1970s, which was an innovative and influential period in American film, notably in the San Francisco Bay Area, where he was based.

I vividly recall my impressions of Hiro's work when I viewed *Never Cry Wolf* at the Art Theatre on East Eighth Street in Greenwich Village, New York. Like everyone who has seen the film, I was impressed with the natural light, the intuitive way the animals and nature were photographed, and the respect for the characters in the film. I remember thinking that if I were going to make a film, I would like to work with Hiro Narita.

When I was developing *The Inland Sea*, it was very natural to work with Hiro. Although he worked in American feature films, he was originally from Japan, and not only did I want to work with someone whose aesthetics bridged both cultures, his work fit our film perfectly. *The Inland Sea* is based on the Japan travel memoir by Donald Richie, and we returned to shoot in the rural islands Donald described, mixing the senses of past and present. What is distinctive about shooting with Hiro is combination of kindness, precision, and art. We were making an on-the-fly documentary, and you can see in our film the fluid utilization of movement (in ferries, cars, and trains), the lyrical interplay of light on the water, sensitivity to people in their surroundings, and a natural elegance in framing. Added to all this was an appreciation of architecture and an empathetic relationship to animals. I was privileged to work with Hiro again on my documentary about Antonin Dvorak In New York and Iowa (*Dvorak and America*). Once again, shooting in 16mm film and operating his own camera, Hiro brought to life the profound awe of nature Dvorak experienced as he was composing his music.

Many words will be written about Hiro Narita's contributions to American feature films, but his work on intimate documentaries shows a different side to his art. I'm grateful to have worked with him, and to have learned from him.

Eleanor Coppola

Hiro Narita was a superb cinematographer for my short movie *Love is Love is Love*. I am not a director who gives shot lists. We had discussions about the look and feel of the movie, the story, and emotions. Hiro had to translate our conversations into visual images. He is a remarkable talent with a lifetime of experience to draw from, and he had a creative solution for every situation that arose. His quiet, observant, calm personality was the perfect complement to the 10 strong women actors in the movie.

Lynn Hershman Leeson

It is difficult to not write in superlatives about Hiro Narita's superb talents. I am fortunate to have worked with him for over twenty-five years when he was the cinematographer on a wide range of projects from feature films to documentaries to art installations. During this time, I witnessed first-hand the remarkable dimensions of his refined perspective. Hiro consistently combines his elegant vision with an extraordinary array of techniques, all of which are both inventive and disciplined. Hiro's ability to transform what might have been ordinary footage into astonishing, original shots that convey a deep and profound subtext of meaning is unparalleled.

Scott Farrar, ASC

I met Hiro Narita during the production of *Star Trek VI: The Undiscovered Country*, in 1991. And we've been friends ever since. During pre-production all the HOD's (heads of department) go through the script, plan the shots, visit locations, create the sets and get to know one another. That's when I got to know Hiro. As visual effects supervisor I usually spent a lot of time working with the director of photography so that our effects work would blend seamlessly with the lighting style of the movie. It was immediately very easy to talk with Hiro and make our plans. He struck me as a man with artist's sensibilities, especially talented in the use of lighting, composition, and color. I recall that any problems we ran into, Hiro handled them with a calm and measured approach. Making a movie is always challenging hard work. But Hiro, with his knowledge and talent, made the film look great.
I have fond memories of that project, and of working with Hiro. We had a lot of fun and the VFX shots we did with him looked really cool!

Bruce Nicholson
Former VFX Supervisor at ILM
Independent Filmmaker

Although Hiro Narita has spent most of his film career as a live action cameraman, he also did his share of second unit and visual effects cinematography. I met Hiro at ILM during post-production of *Return of the Jedi*, where he was shooting some vfx elements. Over the years, we worked together on a number of projects: Jedi, Indiana Jones & the Temple of Doom, Always, commercials for Panasonic, and a smattering of other projects. Hiro made a huge contribution to Always as second unit DP. Because most of the miniature aircraft effects were done in camera, it took someone with Hiro's experience and artistry to create astonishingly believable shots. And because Steven Spielberg was directing this picture, the bar was set very high. Hiro went on to DP many other feature films. He has also applied his skills to the short independent films that I've been making in recent years, doing camera work and helping to shape the narrative. It is a testament to Hiro's character: No project is too big or small for his contributions!

Filmography

Cinematographer

Logic Paralyzes the Heart (2022, Short)
Director: Lynn Hershman Leeson Starring: Joan Chen

Love Is Love Is Love (2020)
Segment - Late Lunch
Director: Eleanor Coppola Screenplay/Story: Eleanor Coppola, Karen Leigh Hopkins Starring: Cybill Shepherd, Rita Wilson, Alyson Reed, Maya Kazan Film Editing: Robert Schafer Music: Laura Karpman

Tania Libre (2017, Documentary)
Director: Lynn Hershman Leeson Starring: Tania Bruguera, Frank Ochberg, Tilda Swinton (Narrator-voice)

VertiGhost (2017, Short)
Director: Lynn Hershman Leeson Screenplay/Story: Lynn Hershman Leeson

Love & Taxes (2015)
Director: Jacob Kornbluth Screenplay/Story: Josh Kornbluth Starring: Robert Reich, Harry Shearer, Warren Keith, Sarah Overman Film Editing: Lisa Fruchtman, Rick LeCompte Music: Marco D'Ambrosio

La Mission (2009)
Director: Peter Bratt Screenplay/Story: Peter Bratt Starring: Ben-

filmography

jamin Bratt, Jeremy Ray Valdez, Talisa Soto, Jesse Borrego Film Editing: Stan Webb Music: Mark Kilian

A Perfect Place (2008, Short)
Director: Derrick Scocchera Screenplay/Story: Derrick Scocchera Starring: Mark Boone Junior, Bill Moseley, Todd Lookinland, Isabelle Maynard Film Editing: Derrick Scocchera Music: Mike Patton

Strange Culture (2007, Documentary)
Director: Lynn Hershman Leeson Screenplay/Story: Lynn Hershman Leeson Starring: Thomas Jay Ryan, Tilda Swinton, Peter Coyote, Josh Kornbluth Film Editing: Lynn Hershman-Leeson Music: The Residents

Valley of the Heart's Delight (2006)
Director: Tim Boxell Screenplay/Story: Miles Murphy Starring: Pete Postlethwaite, Gabriel Mann, Diana Scarwid, Bruce McGill Film Editing: Jay Boekelheide Music: Richard Gibbs, Nicholas O'Toole

The Darwin Awards (2006)
Director: Finn Taylor Screenplay/Story: Finn Taylor Starring: Joseph Fiennes, Winona Ryder, Lawrence Ferlinghetti, Juliette Lewis Film Editing: Rick LeCompte Music: David Kitay

Night of Henna (2005)
Director: Hassan Zee Screenplay/Story: Hassan Zee Starring: Girija Shankar, Pooja Kumar, Nancy Carlin Film Editing: Sharon Franklin, J.D. Sievertson Music: George Gousis, Chebbi Sabah, Water Music

Teknolust (2002)
Director: Lynn Hershman Leeson Screenplay/Story: Lynn Hershman Leeson Starring: Tilda Swinton, Jeremy Davies, Karen Black Film Editing: Lisa Fruchtman Music: Klaus Badelt, Mark Tschanz

Other People (2001, TV Movie)
Director: Michael W. Watkins Starring: Max Barrie, Monnae Michaell, Warren Sweeney

Dvorak and America (2000, Documentary)
Director: Lucille Carra Screenplay/Story: Lucille Carra Film Editing: Brian Cotnoir

Gilmore Girls (2000, TV Series)
Episode – Pilot
Director: Lesli Linka Glatter Screenplay/Story: Amy Sherman-Palladino Starring: Lauren Graham, Alexis Bledel, Keiko Agena, Scott Patterson Film Editing: Jill Savitt Music: Sam Phillips

Dirty Pictures (2000, TV Movie)
Director: Frank Pierson Screenplay/Story: Ilene Chaiken Starring: James Woods, Craig T. Nelson, Diana Scarwid, Susan Sarandon Film Editing: Peter Zinner Music: Mark Snow

Fortress 2: Re-entry (1999)
Director: Geoff Murphy Screenplay/Story: Steven Feinberg, Troy Neighbors, John Flock, Peter Doyle Starring: Christopher Lambert, David Roberson, Liz May Brice, Pam Grier Film Editing: James R. Symons Music: Christopher Franke

Partners (1999, TV Series)
Episode - Pilot
Director: Carl Franklin Starring: Melissa Sue Anderson, Amanda Peet, Lochlyn Munro, Wendy Moniz, Andy Arness

I'll Be Home for Christmas (1998)
Director: Arlene Sanford Screenplay/Story: Tom Nursall, Harris Goldberg, Michael Allin Starring: Jonathan Taylor Thomas, Jessica Biel, Eve Gordon Film Editing: Anita Brandt Burgoyne Music: John Debney

Shadrach (1998)
Director: Susanna Styron Screenplay/Story: William Styron, Susanna Styron, Bridget Terry Starring: Andie MacDowell, Harvey Keitel, Martin Sheen (Narrator- voice) Film Editing: Colleen Sharp Music: Van Dyke Parks

Sub Down (1997)
Director: Gregg Champion Screenplay/Story: Silvio Muraglia, Daniel Sladek, Howard Chesley, Howard Chesley Starring: Stephen Baldwin, Tom Conti, Gabrielle Anwar Film Editing: Cary Shott Music: Stefano Mainetti

Sub Down: from back left, Silvio Muraglia, Severino Tramontani, Hiro Narita, Lucianino Giusepponi, Marco Sticchi, unidentified, sitting Alessandro Bolognesi, Maurizio Cremisini on the set in Luxemburg

Conceiving Ada (1997)
Director: Lynn Hershman Leeson Screenplay/Story: Lynn Hershman Leeson, Eileen Jones, Sadie Plant, Betty A. Toole Starring: Tilda Swinton, Karen Black, Timothy Leary Film Editing: Robert Dalva Music:The Residents

Visas and Virtue (1997, Short)
Director: Chris Tashima Screenplay/Story: Tom Donaldson, Chris Tashima, Tim Toyama Starring: Chris Tashima, Diana Georger, Susan Fukuda Film Editing: Irvin Paik Music: Scott Nagatani

American Masters (1997, TV Series documentary)
Episode - Isamu Noguchi: Stones and Paper Director: Hiro Narita Screenplay/Story: Sharon Wood Starring: Christo, Linda Hunt (Narrator), Isamu Noguchi, I.M. Pei Film Editing: William Smock Music: Larry London

James and the Giant Peach (1996)
Director: Henry Selick Screenplay/Story: Roald Dahl, Karey Kirkpatrick, Jonathan Roberts, Steve Bloom Starring: Pete Postlethwaite, Paul Terry, Miriam Margolyes, Joanna Lumley Film Editing: Stan Webb Music by Randy Newman (cinematography / live action)

The Arrival (1996)
Director: David Twohy Screenplay/Story: David Twohy Starring: Charlie Sheen, Ron Silver, Lindsay Crouse, Teri Polo Film Editing: Martin Hunter Music: Arthur Kempel

Long Shadows (1994, TV Movie)
Director: Sheldon Larry Screenplay/Story: Milan Stitt Starring: Matt Frewer, Fumi Dan, Elizabeth Ruscio Film Editing: Angelo Corrao Music: Peter Manning Robinson

White Fang II: Myth of the White Wolf (1994)
Director: Ken Olin Screenplay/Story: David Fallon Starring: Alfred Molina, Scott Bairstow, Charmaine Craig, Geoffrey Lewis Film Editing: Elba Sanchez-Short Music: John Debney

Siegfried & Roy: The Magic and Mystery (1994)
Director: Charles A. Bangert Screenplay/Story: Louis H. Gorfain Starring: Ron Foster (narrator), Siegfried Fischbacher, Roy Horn Film Editing: Hank O'Karma Music: Arthur Kempel

filmography

They / Children of Mist (1993, TV Movie)
Director: John Korty Screenplay/Story: Rudyard Kipling, Edithe Swensen Starring: Vanessa Redgrave, Patrick Bergin, Rutanya Alda Film Editing: Jim Oliver Music: Gerald Gouriet

Hocus Pocus (1993)
Director: Kenny Ortega Screenplay/Story: David Kirschner, Mick Garris, Neil Cuthbert Starring: Bette Midler, Sarah Jessica Parker, Kathy Najimy, Charles Rocket Film Editing: Peter E. Berger Music: John Debney

Gunmen (1993)
Director: Deran Sarafian Screenplay/Story: Stephen Sommers Starring: Christopher Lambert, Mario Van Peebles, Patrick Stewart, Sally Kirkland, Richard C. Sarafian Film Editing: Bonnie Koehler Music: John Debney

Tales from the Crypt (1992, TV Series)
Episode - Showdown
Director: Richard Donner Screenplay/Story: Frank Darabont, Steven Dodd Starring: David Morse, Neil Giuntoli, Paul T. Murray Film Editing: Stephen Semel Music: Michael Kamen

Star Trek VI: The Undiscovered Country (1991)
Director: Nicholas Meyer Screenplay/Story: Gene Roddenberry, Leonard Nimoy, Lawrence Konner, Mark Rosenthal, Nicholas Meyer, Denny Martin Flinn Starring: William Shatner, Leonard Nimoy, DeForest Kelley, James Doohan, Walter Koenig, Nichelle Nichols, George Takei Film Editing: William Hoy, Ronald Roose Music: Cliff Eidelman

The Inland Sea (1991)
Director: Lucille Carra Screenplay/Story: Donald Richie, Lucille Carra Starring: Donald Richie (Narrator -voice), Keijo Hasegawa, Akira Hamada, Tasuya Hatanaka Film Editing: Brian Cotnoir Music: Tôru Takemitsu

The Rocketeer (1991)
Director: Joe Johnston Screenplay/Story: Dave Stevens, Paul De Meo, William Dear, Danny Bilson Starring: Billy Campbell, Jennifer Connelly, Timothy Dalton, Alan Arkin Paul Sorvino Film Editing: Arthur Schmidt Music: James Horner

Plymouth (1991, TV Movie)
Director: Lee David Zlotoff Screenplay/Story: Lee David Zlotoff Starring: Cindy Pickett, Richard Hamilton, Perrey Reeves, James Rebhorn, Jerry Hardin Film Editing: O. Nicholas Brown, John W. Wheeler Music: Brad Fiedel

Roller Coaster Rabbit (1990, short)
Directors: Rob Minkoff & (live action seq) Frank Marshall Screenplay/Story: Gary K. Wolf, Bill Kopp, Kevin Harkey, Lynne Naylor, Patrick A. Ventura Starring: Charles Fleischer (voice), Kathleen Turner (voice), April Winchell (voice), Lou Hirsch (voice), Corey Burton (voice), Frank Welker (voice), Damian London, Joni Barnes Film Editing: Chuck Williams Music: Bruce Broughton (cinematography / live action seq)

Mothers, Daughters and Lovers (1989, TV Movie)
Director: Matthew Robbins Screenplay/Story: Willard Huyck, Gloria Katz Starring: Claude Akins, Jim Beaver, Ellen Dolan Film Editing: Glenn Farr, Fred Roth, Michael Tronick Music: Tom Scott

Honey, I Shrunk the Kids (1989)
Director: Joe Johnston Screenplay/Story: Ed Naha, Tom Schulman, Stuart Gordon, Brian Yuzna Starring: Rick Moranis, Matt Frewer, Kristine Sutherland, Marcia Strassman, Carl Steven Film Editing: Michael A. Stevenson Music: James Horner

Shuttlecock (1989)
Director: Jerry Barrish Screenplay/Story: Jerry Barrish, Betsy Brown, Christa Maerker Starring: Will Durst, Liane Hielscher, Jim Bowyer Music: Richard Secrist

filmography

Tummy Trouble (1989, short)
Directors: Rob Minkoff & (live action seq) Frank Marshall Screenplay/Story: Kevin Harkey, Bill Kopp, Rob Minkoff, Mark Kausler, Patrick A. Ventura Starring: Charles Fleischer (voice), Kathleen Turner (voice), April Winchell (voice), Lou Hirsch (voice), Corey Burton (voice), Frank Welker (voice), Sol Pavlovsky, Charles Noland Film Editing: Donald W. Ernst Music: James Horner (cinematography / live action seq)

American Playhouse (1988, TV Series)
Episode Pigeon Feathers
Director: Sharron Miller Screenplay/Story: Jan Hartman, John Updike Starring: Christopher Collet, Caroline McWilliams, Jeffrey DeMunn Film Editing: Rachel Igel, Sharron Miller Music: David Amram

No Man's Land (1987)
Director: Peter Werner Screenplay/Story: Dick Wolf Starring: Charlie Sheen, Randy Quaid, Bill Duke, Lara Harris Film Editing: Steven Cohen, Daniel P. Hanley Music: Basil Poledouris

Amerika (1987, TV Mini Series -7 episodes)
Director: Donald Wrye Screenplay/Story: Donald Wrye Starring: Kris Kristofferson, Sam Neill, Lara Flynn Boyle, Mariel Hemingway Film Editing: Martin Cohen, Frank Mazzola, Michael Ripps, Craig Bassett, Raja Gosnell, Dan Harville, Jacque Elaine Toberen Music: Basil Poledouris

Fire with Fire (1986)
Director: Duncan Gibbins Screenplay/Story: Bill Phillips, Warren Skaaren, Paul Boorstin, Sharon Boorstin Starring: Craig Sheffer, Virginia Madsen, Jon Polito Film Editing: Peter E. Berger Music: Howard Shore

Prince Jack (1985)
Director: Bert Lovitt Screenplay/Story: Bert Lovitt Starring: Rob-

ert Hogan, Dana Andrews, Jim Backus, Theodore Bikel Film Editing: Janice Hampton Music: Elmer Bernstein

The Blue Yonder (1985, TV Movie)
Director: Mark Rosman Screenplay/Story: Mark Rosman
Starring: Peter Coyote, Huckleberry Fox, Art Carney Film editing: Betsy Blankett Milicevic Music: David Shire

Sylvester (1985)
Director: Tim Hunter Screenplay/Story: Carol Sobieski Starring: Richard Farnsworth, Melissa Gilbert, Constance Towers Film Editing: David Garfield, Suzanne Pettit, Howard E. Smith Music Lee Holdridge

American Playhouse (1985, TV Series)
Episode Go Tell It on the Mountain
Director: Stan Lathan Screenplay/Story: James Baldwin, Gus Edwards, Leslie Lee Starring: Paul Winfield, Olivia Cole, Ruby Dee, Ving Rhames Film Editing: Jay Freund Music: Webster Lewis

American Playhouse (1984, TV Series)
Episode Solomon Northup's Odyssey
Director: Gordon Parks Screenplay/Story: Solomon Northup, Lou Potter, Samm-Art Williams Starring: Avery Brooks, Rhetta Greene, Mason Adams, Lee Bryant, Art Evans, John Saxon, Joe Seneca Film Editing: John Carter Music: Gordon Parks

The Haunting Passion (1983, TV Movie)
Director: John Korty Screenplay/Story: Michael Berk, Douglas Schwartz Starring: Jane Seymour, Gerald McRaney, Ruth Nelson, Millie Perkins Film Editing: Peter Kirby Music: Paul Chihara

Never Cry Wolf (1983)
Director: Carroll Ballard Screenplay/Story: Farley Mowat, Curtis Hanson, Sam Hamm, Richard Kletter, Charles Martin Smith, Eugene Corr, Christina Luescher, Ralph Furmaniak, Jay Presson

filmography

Allen, Starring: Charles Martin Smith, Brian Dennehy, Zachary Ittimannag, Samsom Jorah Film Editing: Michael Chandler, Peter Parasheles Music: Mark Isham

The Stereo Demonstration Film (1982, Short)
Director: Andy Aaron Starring: Tony Hartford, Hugh Fraser, Theresa Bramnick, Lee Simon Film Editing: Gerald B. Greenberg Music: Philip Aaberg, Wendy Carlos, Kenneth Gundry

Nanette: An Aside (1977, TV Movie)
Director: Rik van Glintenkamp Screenplay/Story: Willa Cather, Rik van Glintenkamp Starring: Kola Kwariani, Donna Mitchell, Carolyn Mignini Film Editing: Deborah Wallach, Rick Wilson Music: Michael Hoppe

Farewell to Manzanar (1976, TV Movie)
Director: John Korty Screenplay/Story: Jeanne Houston, James D. Houston, John Korty Starring: Yuki Shimoda, Pat Morita, Nobu McCarthy, James Saito Film Editing: Eric Albertson Music: Paul Chihara

He Is My Brother (1975)
Director: Edward Dmytryk Screenplay/Story: James Polakof, David Pritchard Starring: Bobby Sherman, Kathy Paulo, Keenan Wynn Film Editing: Vivien Hillgrove Music: Ed Bogas

Memory of us (1974)
Director: H. Kaye Dyal Screenplay/Story: Ellen Geer
Starring: Will Geer, Ellen Geer, Jon Cypher Film Editing: Harry Keramidas Music: Ed Bogas
(as Hiro Morikawa)

Silence (1974)
Director: John Korty Screenplay/Story: Ellen Geer, Mary Mackey Starring: Will Geer, Ellen Geer, Richard Kelton Film Editing: Vivien Hillgrove Music: Ed Bogas
(as Hiro Morikawa)

hiro narita. depth of field

Camera operator / additional camera operator:

Shrink Rap (2007, TV Series)
Episode - Robin Williams
Director: Michael Waldman Starring: Robin Williams, Pamela Stephenson Editor: Alex Broad Music: Simon Heath (camera operator as Hiro Narito)

American Experience (2005, TV Series)
Episode The Fall of Saigon
Director: Elizabeth Deane Screenplay/Story: Elizabeth Deane Starring: Stanley Karnow, Will Lyman (Narrator) Film Editing: Daniel Eisenberg, Carol Hayward Music: Mickey Hart (camera operator)

Indiana Jones and the Temple of Doom (1984)
Director: Steven Spielberg Screenplay/Story: Willard Huyck, Gloria Katz, George Lucas Starring: Harrison Ford, Kate Capshaw, Dan Aykroyd, Ke Huy Quan, Amrish Puri Cinematography: Douglas Slocombe Film Editing: Michael Kahn, George Lucas Music: John Williams (additional camera operator)

The Right Stuff (1983)
Director: Philip Kaufman Screenplay/Story: Philip Kaufman, Tom Wolfe Starring: Sam Shepard, Scott Glenn, Ed Harris, Dennis Quaid, Fred Ward, Barbara Hershey Cinematography: Caleb Deschanel Film Editing: Glenn Farr, Lisa Fruchtman, Tom Rolf Stephen A. Rotter, Douglas Stewart Music: Bill Conti (additional camera operator)

Vietnam: A Television History (1983, TV Mini Series documentary)
Episode The End of the Tunnel: 1973-1975
Director: Elizabeth Deane Screenplay/Story: Starring: Elizabeth Deane Diem Bui, Tin Bui, Gerald Ford, Henry Kissinger Film Editing: Daniel Eisenberg, Carol Hayward Music: George Gousis, Mickey Hart, Bill Kreutzmann (camera operator)

filmography

Human Highway (1982)
Directors: Dean Stockwell & Neil Young Screenplay/Story: Neil Young Jeanne Field, Dean Stockwell, Russ Tamblyn, James Beshears Starring: Neil Young, Russ Tamblyn, Dean Stockwell, Dennis Hopper, Sally Kirkland Cinematography: David Myers Film Editing: James Beshears (camera operator: dream sequence)

Shadows and Light (1980, Video documentary)
Director: Joni Mitchell Starring: Joni Mitchell, Don Alias, Pat Metheny, Jaco Pastorius Cinematography: David Myers Film Editing: Calli Cerami, Joni Mitchell Music: Frankie Lymon, Pat Metheny, Charles Mingus, Joni Mitchell, Jaco Pastorius (camera operator)

More American Graffiti (1979)
Director: Bill Norton Screenplay/Story: Bill Norton, George Lucas, Gloria Katz, Willard Huyck Starring: Ron Howard, Candy Clark, Bo Hopkins, Paul Le Mat, Mackenzie Phillips, Charles Martin Smith, Scott Glenn Film Editing: Tina Hirsch, Duwayne Dunham, Marcia Lucas Music: Eugene Finley, George Lucas (camera operator)

Apocalypse Now (1979)
Director: Francis Ford Coppola Screenplay/Story: John Milius, Francis Ford Coppola, Michael Herr, Joseph Conrad Starring: Marlon Brando, Martin Sheen, Robert Duvall, Frederic Forrest, Laurence Fishburne, Harrison Ford, Dennis Hopper Cinematography: Vittorio Storaro AIC-ASC Film Editing: Lisa Fruchtman, Gerald B. Greenberg, Walter Murch Music: Carmine Coppola, Francis Ford Coppola (camera operator: insert)

The Bee Gees Special (1979)
Director: Louis J. Horvitz Screenplay/Story: Stuart Birnbaum, Ken Ehrlich Starring: Barry Gibb, Robin Gibb, Maurice Gibb, Andy Gibb, Willie Nelson Cinematography: Stephen H. Burum ASC Film Editing: Harvey Berger, Bill Breshears, Tony Hayman (additional camera operator)

hiro narita. depth of field

The Candidate (1972)
Director: Michael Ritchie Screenplay/Story: Jeremy Larner Starring: Robert Redford, Peter Boyle, Melvyn Douglas, Don Porter Cinematography: Victor J. Kemper Film Editing: Robert Estrin, Richard A. Harris Music: John Rubinstein (additional camera operator)

Zabriskie Point (1969)
Director: Michelangelo Antonioni Screenplay/Story: Michelangelo Antonioni, Franco Rossetti, Sam Shepard, Tonino Guerra, Clare People Starring: Mark Frechette, Daria Halprin, Rod Taylor Cinematography: Alfio Contini AIC Film Editing: Franco Arcalli, Michelangelo Antonioni Music: Jerry Garcia, Pink Floyd (additional camera operator)

Additional Cinematography

Women Art Revolution (2010)
Director: Lynn Hershman Leeson Starring: Lynn Hershman Leeson, B. Ruby Rich Film Editing: Lynn Hershman Leeson (additional cinematography with cinematographers Antonio Rossi, Fawn Yacker, Lise Swenson, Lynn Hershman)

Half Past Autumn: The Life and Works of Gordon Parks (2000, TV Movie documentary)
Director: Craig Laurence Rice Screenplay/Story: Lou Potter Starring: Gordon Parks, Isaac Hayes, Nelson George Film Editing: Sam Pollard Music: Mario Sprouse (additional cinematography with cinematographers Henry Adebonojo, Greg Andracke, Brian Sewell)

Dream of the Sea Ranch (1994)
Director: Zara Muren Screenplay/Story: Zara Muren Starring: Al Boeke, Lawrence Halprin, Joseph Esherick, Charles Moore Cinematography: Zara Muren Film Editing: Zara Muren

filmography

The Unbearable Lightness of Being (1988)
Director: Philip Kaufman Screenplay/Story: Milan Kundera, Jean-Claude Carrière, Philip Kaufman Starring: Daniel Day-Lewis, Juliette Binoche, Lena Olin, Erland Josephson Cinematography: Sven Nykvist Film Editing: Vivien Hillgrove, Michael Magill, Walter Murch, B.J. Sears Music: Mark Adler (Cinematography / US unit)

Nutcracker (1986)
Director: Carroll Ballard Screenplay/Story: Kent Stowell, Maurice Sendak, E.T.A. Hoffmann Starring: Hugh Duncan Bigney Mitchell, Vanessa Sharp, Wade Walthall, Patricia Barker Cinematography: Stephen H. Burum Film Editing: John Nutt, Michael Silvers Music: Mark Adler (additional cinematography)

Blue Velvet (1986)
Director: David Lynch Screenplay/Story: David Lynch Starring: Kyle MacLachlan, Isabella Rossellini, Dennis Hopper, Laura Dern Cinematography: Frederick Elmes Film Editing: Duwayne Dunham Music: Angelo Badalamenti (additional cinematography - uncredited)

Crackers (1984)
Director: Louis Malle Screenplay/Story: Jeffrey Alan Fiskin Starring: Donald Sutherland, Jack Warden, Sean Penn, Wallace Shawn Cinematography: László Kovács HSC ASC Film Editing: Suzanne Baron Music: Paul Chihara

Return of the Jedi (1983)
Director: Richard Marquand Screenplay/Story: Lawrence Kasdan, George Lucas Starring: Mark Hamill, Harrison Ford, Carrie Fisher, Billy Dee Williams, Anthony Daniels, Peter Mayhew Cinematography: Alan Hume, Alec Mills Film Editing: Sean Barton, T.M. Christopher, Duwayne Dunham, Marcia Lucas, George Lucas Music: John Williams (additional cinematography uncredited)

hiro narita. depth of field

Gospel (1983)
Directors: David Leivick, Frederick A. Ritzenberg
Starring: James Cleveland, Walter Hawkins, Twinkie Clark,
Shirley Caesar Cinematography: David Myers Film Editing: Glenn
Farr Music: Miles Goodman (additional cinematography)

Mr. Adler and the opera (1982)
Director: Eugene Finley (additional cinematography)

Rust Never Sleeps (1979)
Director: Neil Young Starring: Neil Young, Ralph Molina, Frank
'Pancho' Sampedro, Billy Talbot Film Editing: Neil Young (additional cinematography with cinematographers Jon Else, Paul Goldsmith, Robbie Greenberg, L.A. Johnson, David Myers, Richard Pearce)

The Last Waltz (1978, Documentary)
Director: Martin Scorsese Screenplay/Story: Mardik Martin Starring: Robbie Robertson, Muddy Waters, Neil Young, Van Morrison, Neil Diamond, Bob Dylan, Joni Mitchell, Eric Clapton Cinematography: Michael Chapman Film Editing: Jan Roblee, Yeu-Bun Yee (additional cinematography with László Kovács, Bobby Byrne, David Myers Michael W. Watkins, Vilmos Zsigmond)

Who'll Stop the Rain (1978)
Director: Karel Reisz Screenplay/Story: Robert Stone, Judith Rascoe, Robert Stone Starring: Nick Nolte, Tuesday Weld, Michael Moriarty, Anthony Zerbe Cinematography: Richard H. Kline Music: Laurence Rosenthal (additional cinematography)

Cinematography: second unit

Anger Management (2003)
Director: Peter Segal Screenplay/Story: David Dorfman
Starring: Adam Sandler, Jack Nicholson, Marisa Tomei, Woody

Harrelson, John Turturro Cinematography: Donald McAlpine Film Editing: Jeff Gourson Music: Teddy Castellucci (Cinematography: second unit)

The Scorpion King (2002)
Director: Chuck Russell Screenplay/Story: William Osborne, David Hayter, Stephen Sommers, Jonathan Hales Starring: Dwayne Johnson, Steven Brand, Michael Clarke Duncan, Kelly Hu Cinematography: John R. Leonetti Film Editing: Greg Parsons, Michael Tronick Music: John Debney (Cinematography: second unit)

The Time Machine (2002)
Director: Simon Wells Screenplay/Story: H.G. Wells, David Duncan, John Logan Starring: Guy Pearce, Jeremy Irons, Phyllida Law, Yancey Arias, Mark Addy Cinematography: Donald McAlpine Film Editing: Wayne Wahrman Music: Klaus Badelt (Cinematography: second unit)

Simon Birch (1998)
Director: Mark Steven Johnson Screenplay/Story: Mark Steven Johnson, John Irving Starring: Ashley Judd, Jim Carrey, Oliver Platt, David Strathairn Cinematography: Aaron Schneider Film Editing: David Finfer Music: Marc Shaiman (Cinematography: second unit)

Assistant camera

Riverrun (1968)
Director: John Korty Screenplay/Story: Bill Brammer, John Korty Starring: Mark Jenkins, John McLiam, George Hellyer Jr. Cinematography: John Korty Film Editing: Paddy Monk Music: Peter Berg, Richard Greene

Visual consultant

Generic Thriller (2009)
Director: Scott Sublett Screenplay/Story: Scott Sublett
Starring: Daniel Hart Donoghue, Rosemary Griggs, Shirley Jones
Film Editing: Jay Boekelheide, Mark Tran Music: Aaron J. Goldstein

All About Dad (2009)
Director: Mark Tran Screenplay/Story: Mark Tran Starring: David Huynh, Nanrisa Lee, Yvonne Truong Cinematography: Todd Banhazl Film Editing: Jeremy Castillo Music: Ryan Rey

Visual effects cinematography

Always (1989)
Director: Steven Spielberg Screenplay/Story: Jerry Belson, Dalton Trumbo, Frederick Hazlitt Brennan, Chandler Sprague, David Boehm Starring: Richard Dreyfuss, Holly Hunter, Brad Johnson, John Goodman, Audrey Hepburn Cinematography: Mikael Salomon Film Editing: Michael Kahn Music: John Williams (miniature unit)

Second Unit Director

Anger Management (2003)
Director: Peter Segal Screenplay/Story: David Dorfman
Starring: Adam Sandler, Jack Nicholson, Marisa Tomei, Woody Harrelson, John Turturro Cinematography: Donald McAlpine Film Editing: Jeff Gourson Music: Teddy Castellucci (second unit director: New York)

filmography

Always (1989). Miniature night forest fire with the fire fighting aircraft. Hiro Narita, left on the camera car roof, with camera operator Kim Marks and special effect supervisor Robert Finley in front. Photo courtesy of ILM

Director

American Masters (1997, TV Series documentary)
Episode - Isamu Noguchi: Stones and Paper
Screenplay/Story: Sharon Wood Starring: Christo, Linda Hunt (Narrator), Isamu Noguchi, I.M. Pei Cinematography: Hiro Narita Film Editing: William Smock Music: Larry London

Self

Cinematographer Style (2006)
Director: Jon Fauer Screenplay/Story: Volker Bahnemann, Jon Fauer Cinematography: Jon Fauer, Brian Heller, Jeffrey Laszlo, David Morgan Film Editing: Matthew R. Blute Music: Christian Bischoff, Florian Schlagbauer, Thomas Schlagbauer

Awards & Nominations

Awards:

Boston International Film Festival
2006   Best Cinematography for Valley of the Heart's Delight (2006)
Cable ACE Awards
1987   Best cinematography for The Blue Yonder (1985)
Boston Society of Film Critics Awards
1984   BSFC Award Best Cinematography for Never Cry Wolf (1983)
National Society of Film Critics Awards, USA
1984   NSFC Award Best Cinematography for Never Cry Wolf (1983)
Hawaii International Film Festival
1984   Excellence in Cinematography Award

Nominations:

Primetime Emmy Awards
2001   Outstanding Cinematography for Non-Fiction Programming Half Past Autumn: The Life and Works of Gordon Parks (2000)
2000   Outstanding Cinematography for a Miniseries, Movie or a Special Dirty Pictures (2000)
1976   Outstanding Achievement in Cinematography for Entertainment Programming for a Special Farewell to Manzanar (1976)

Los Angeles Film Critics Association Awards
1983   LAFCA Award Best Cinematography for Never Cry Wolf (1983)

New York Film Critics Circle Awards
1983   NYFCC Award Best Cinematographer for Never Cry Wolf (1983)

Membership

International Photographers Guild
American Society Cinematographers (ASC)
Academy Motion Picture Arts and Sciences

Artdigiland is an international and multilingual publishing project committed spreading the word of selected contemporary artists. And essays, monographs, materials, literary works.

Artdigiland is also a web community consisting of authors, editors, filmmakers. Visit our blog: https://www.artdigiland.com/blog.

Subscribe to our newsletter to be advised about new releases, events and offers reserved for our readers: http://www.artdigiland.com/newsl

http://artdigiland.com

info: www.artdigiland.com

contact: info@artdigiland.com

interview with Marc Scialom
edited by Silvia Tarquini

interview with Fabrizio Crisafulli
edited by Enzo Cillo

interview with Beppe Lanci
edited by Monica Pollini

interview with Ugo Gregoretti
edited by Vincenzo Valentino

interview with Eugene Green
edited by Federico Francioni

interview with Luca Bigazzi
edited by Alberto Spadafora

interview with Adriana Berselli
edited by Vittoria C. Caratozzolo,
Silvia Tarquini

interview with Salvatore Mereu
edited by Franca Farina

interview with Luciano Tovoli
edited by Piercesare Stagni
e Valentina Valente

Artdigiland publishes, in several languages, a series dedicated to the artistic use of the light in cinema and theatre:

LUCE DEL NOSTRO TEMPO
Conversazioni con venti autori della fotografia sul cinema italiano contemporaneo,
a cura di Ludovico Cantisani e Tobia Cimini,
prefazione di Silvia Tarquini, postfazione di Pedro Armocida, 2022

Questo libro è allo stesso tempo una riflessione sul cinema italiano contemporaneo dell'ultimo decennio e un'indagine sull'arte degli autori della fotografia e sul loro particolare statuto di interpreti e realizzatori, *attraverso la luce*, delle scelte del regista. In un ristretto numero di film, venti titoli, raccontati dai cinematographers ai curatori del volume, si ri-attraversano alcuni capolavori che hanno segnato l'immaginario di questi anni e si contemplano molti e diversi tipi di approccio alla regia. Tra pellicola e digitale, autori della fotografia quali Renato Berta, Gogò Bianchi, Luca Bigazzi, Nicolaj Brüel, Maurizio Calvesi, Paolo Carnera, Arnaldo Catinari, Sandro Chessa, Daniele Ciprì, Matteo Cocco, Daria D'Antonio, Michele D'Attanasio, Francesco Di Giacomo, Stefano Falivene, Crystel Fournier, Gherardo Gossi, Giuseppe Maio, Ferran Paredes Rubio, Alessandro Pesci e Vladan Radovic raccontano il proprio lavoro. E, come sintetizza perfettamente Renato Berta, ci insegnano che «la libertà esiste solo all'interno di una concezione».

L'EROICO MASINI
Un direttore della fotografia tra Carmelo Bene e i fratelli Taviani
a cura di Ludovico Cantisani d'Auria,
prefazione di Dario Zonta, 2022

Mario Masini, classe 1939, iniziato al cinema da padre David Maria Turoldo e diplomatosi al Centro Sperimentale di Cinematografia, si è ritagliato un posto d'eccezione come direttore della fotografia e come regista nel cinema underground e sperimentale romano degli anni '60 e '70, firmando *X chiama Y* (1967). Tra il 1968 e il 1973 ha fotografato quattro dei cinque film della parentesi cinematografica di Carmelo Bene, *Nostra Signora dei Turchi*, Leone d'argento alla Mostra del Cinema di Venezia, *Don Giovanni*, *Salomè* e *Un Amleto di meno*. Nella sua "Autobiografia" Bene definì Masini "eroico", per gli sforzi compiuti nella realizzazione anarchica di *Nostra Signora dei Turchi* e degli altri film girati insieme, e ancora: «un genio della macchina da presa, che dopo aver lasciato la vita nei miei film, ha pensato bene di cambiar mestiere». In seguito infatti, dopo aver collaborato, tra l'altro, con i fratelli Taviani per *San Michele aveva un gallo* e *Padre padrone*, Palma d'oro a Cannes nel 1977, Masini ha abbandonato il cinema per entrare nel mondo delle scuole steineriane, salvo ritornare a lavorare, negli anni '90, a film tedeschi, italiani – *Tutto parla di te* di Alina Marazzi –, portoghesi ed etiopi: tra i film fotografati in quest'ultima fase della sua carriera, *Why Buddha?*, back-stage di *Piccolo Buddha* di Bertolucci, diretto da Paolo Brunatto, e *Teza* di Haile Gerima, Leone d'argento a Venezia nel 2007. Testimone privilegiato di un'era di avanguardie, in queste pagine Masini riattraversa la sua straordinaria esperienza artistica, tecnica e umana.

ARCOBALENI DI GRIGI E NUOVI COLORI.
CONVERSAZIONE CON VLADAN RADOVIC
a cura di Ludovico Cantisani,
prefazione di Gianni Canova, 2021

Allievo del leggendario Peppino Rotunno, Vladan Radovic ha esordito nel 2004 con *Saimir* di Francesco Munzi. Il suo percorso prosegue al fianco di registi molto diversi fra loro, con grande apertura e larghi margini di sperimentazione: Virzì e Zanasi Mereu, Dipaola, Bispuri, Costanzo. Negli anni Dieci vince il David di Donatello per la migliore fotografia con un film in digitale, l'opera terza di Munzi *Anime nere*. Radovic poi collabora con il produttore e regista Matteo Rovere, con Sydney Sibilia e il team della Ascent/Groenlandia per film produttivamente innovativi e caratterizzati da una grande esplorazione registica e fotografica, come la trilogia di *Smetto quando voglio* e la serie televisiva *Romulus*. Ed è stato distribuito in tutto il mondo *Il traditore* di Marco Bellocchio. Ripercorrendo la sua carriera, Radovic traccia qui un vero e proprio "state of the art" del cinema italiano contemporaneo.

LUCE SU ALBERTO SORDI!
Alberto Sordi nei ricordi dell'autore della fotografia Sergio D'Offizi
a cura di Gerry Guida,
prefazione di Fabio Melelli, 2020

Tra gli artisti italiani della macchina da presa e della luce, autentici maghi dell'immagine, c'è Sergio D'Offizi, classe 1934. Nell'ambito della sua corposa e articolata filmografia, D'Offizi ha stabilito un rapporto privilegiato con Alberto Sordi, uno dei cineasti che ha maggiormente segnato la storia del nostro cinema, come attore e come regista. Attore immenso e uomo di rara intelligenza, Sordi ha saputo circondarsi di persone che valorizzassero al meglio il suo talento di fustigatore dei costumi patrii, con un'attenzione particolare alla sua immagine e al suo personaggio. Sergio D'Offizi è stato per lui prezioso, fedele, fondamentale collaboratore. Il libro racconta puntualmente la storia di questo sodalizio artistico, le scelte luministiche adottate e l'affiancamento creativo al Sordi regista in opere sia impegnate e profetiche sia intelligentemente esilaranti. Descrivendo anche, tra le righe di una rigorosa relazione professionale, una lunga amicizia, tanto discreta quanto profonda.

IL TRADITORE
Raccontato dall'autore della fotografia Vladan Radovic
a cura di Ludovico Cantisani, 2020
Foto di Francesca Fago, Fabio Lovino, Lia Pasqualino

Il libro, curato da Ludovico Cantisani, a sua volta filmmaker e critico cinematografico, si concentra su *Il traditore* di Marco Bellocchio, indagando le relazioni tra regia e direzione della fotografia e ripercorrendo in dettaglio le tappe della lavorazione del film nelle varie location. Nato a Sarajevo, Radovic si forma al Centro Sperimentale di Cinematografia, esordisce come autore della fotografia nei primi anni Duemila, distinguendosi presto come uno degli artisti della luce più capaci e versatili della sua generazione. Fra i registi con cui ha più volte collaborato, Laura Bispuri, Saverio Costanzo, Francesco Munzi, Matteo Rovere, Sydney Sibilia, Paolo Virzì, Gianni Zanasi. Tre volte candidato ai Nastri d'argento, nel 2015 ha vinto il David di Donatello per la fotografia di *Anime nere* di Munzi, ricevendo una seconda candidatura nel 2017 per *La pazza gioia* di Virzì. Nel 2019 *Il traditore* segna la sua prima collaborazione con Marco Bellocchio, che gli frutta diversi nuovi premi e candidature, tra le quali quella alla Migliore Fotografia del David di Donatello.

Giuseppe Pinori
LA LUCE COME COMPAGNA
Viaggi, incontri, miracoli di un autore della cinematografia
prefazione di Roberto Cicutto, 2019

Giuseppe Pinori ripercorre la sua carriera con un racconto appassionato, dedicato soprattutto agli incontri con i registi, ma non solo. Si parte dall'apprendistato con Fernando Cerchio e dalle avventure con Florestano Vancini, Ansano Giannarelli e Piero Nelli; si passa per i film inchiesta con Cesare Zavattini e Enzo Biagi, l'esordio nel lungometraggio con i fratelli Taviani per *Sotto il segno dello Scorpione*, e l'assidua collaborazione con Valentino Orsini; si attraversa il cinema di genere con maestri quali Lucio Fulci; si scandagliano il cinema d'autore e la relazione regista-direttore della fotografia con Maurizio Costanzo, Luigi Mangini, Samy Pavel, Nanni Moretti, Marco Tullio Giordana, Giuliano Montaldo, Roberto Faenza, Giorgio Albertazzi, Vanna Paoli, Giuliano Biagetti, Claver Salizzato, Romano Scavolini. Luce, ombra, fotografia sono parole d'amore.

SUSPIRIA E DINTORNI
Conversazione con Luciano Tovoli
a cura di Piercesare Stagni e Valentina Valente,
prefazione di Antonio Costa, 2018

Suspiria e dintorni prosegue l'esplorazione Artdigiland nei territori dell'uso artistico della luce e del colore. Luciano Tovoli AIC ASC IMAGO è Autore della cinematografia con registi quali Vittorio De Seta, Michelangelo Antonioni, Dario Argento, Maurice Pialat, Valerio Zurlini, Francis Veber, Andrej Tarkovskij, Ettore Scola, Julie Taymor, Barbet Schroeder e molti altri, ed è creatore della federazione Europea degli Autori della Cinematografia – IMAGO. Il volume intervista ripercorre le tappe della realizzazione di un immortale capolavoro, *Suspiria*, dai test effettuati per la fotografia fino ai processi di stampa, facendoci rivivere un'incredibile avventura estetica. Descrive in dettaglio il making di numerose sequenze, la relazione con il regista, approfondisce le premesse culturali e i riferimenti visivi dell'opera, racconta il contesto delle battaglie per l'innovazione delle tecniche fotografiche negli anni '70. Soprattutto, il libro rivela la passione di Luciano Tovoli per l'arte e la sua instancabile ricerca di un uso espressivo del colore nel cinema.

SUSPIRIA E DINTORNI
Conversazione con Luciano Tovoli
a cura di Piercesare Stagni e Valentina Valente,
prefazione di Antonio Costa, 2018

Di *Suspiria e dintorni* è disponibile la versione ebook.

ON SUSPIRIA AND BEYOND
A Conversation with Cinematographer Luciano Tovoli
edited by Piercesare Stagni and Valentina Valente, 2017

On Suspiria and Beyond is a book-interview with cinematographer Luciano Tovoli AIC ASC, who has collaborated with directors such as Vittorio De Seta, Michelangelo Antonioni, Dario Argento, Maurice Pialat, Valerio Zurlini, Francis Veber, Andrej Tarkovskij, Ettore Scola, Julie Taymor, Barbet Schroeder and many others. Tovoli is also the creator of the European Federation of Cinematographers Imago. The volume retraces all the stages of making Suspiria, from test shots to printing. It describes in detail the making of various sequences, relations with the director, explores the cultural premises of this immortal work and the historical context of the struggle for innovation in the cinematography of the Seventies. Above all, it reveals Luciano Tovoli's passion and tireless search for an expressive use of color in films, providing us with a first-hand experience of an incredible adventure in aesthetics.

ON SUSPIRIA AND BEYOND
A Conversation with Cinematographer Luciano Tovoli
edited by Piercesare Stagni and Valentina Valente, 2017

Di *On Suspiria and Beyond* è disponibile la versione ebook.

LA LUCE COME EMOZIONE
Conversazione con Giuseppe Lanci
a cura di Monica Pollini,
prefazione di Laura Delli Colli, 2017

La voce pacata e l'espressione attenta di Giuseppe Lanci, non di rado accompagnate da sottile e delicato umorismo, condurranno il lettore in un racconto che attraversa, nel vivo del set, oltre cinquant'anni del migliore cinema italiano, e non solo. Dalla formazione al Centro Sperimentale di Cinematografia all'esperienza da operatore di macchina al fianco di Tonino Delli Colli e Franco Di Giacomo, dalle incertezze degli esordi all'immersione nella dimensione unica del cinema di Andrej Tarkovskij per *Nostalghia*, dai sodalizi artistici con Marco Bellocchio, Paolo e Vittorio Taviani, Nanni Moretti agli incontri con Bolognini, Magni, Wertmüller, Von Trotta, Cavani, Del Monte, Greco, Piscicelli, Archibugi, Luchetti, Benigni, Franchi... L'arte e il mestiere del creare la luce e l'impatto visivo del film sono resi con dovizia di particolari tecnici ma sempre nell'ambito di un approccio umanistico, e in un insieme di riflessioni che vanno dai condizionamenti produttivi alle relazioni con gli altri reparti del set e gli attori, fino al tema della "carriera" in generale. L'intervista si sofferma poi sull'ultima passione di Lanci, quella per l'insegnamento.

LA LUCE COME EMOZIONE
Conversazione con Giuseppe Lanci
a cura di Monica Pollini,
prefazione di Laura Delli Colli, 2017

Del volume *La luce come emozione* è disponibile una versione economica di formato ridotto e senza immagini; le immagini sono disponibili per i nostri lettori sul sito Artdigiland, al link indicato nel libro.

NOSTALGHIA
Racconto dell'autore della fotografia Giuseppe Lanci
a cura di Monica Pollini, 2018

Tra le cose che mi hanno stimolato di più parlerei della "fotografia dinamica", qualcosa che non avevo mai visto prima di allora. Consiste nella possibilità di modificare la luce all'interno di un piano sequenza, non per motivi naturalistici – nel senso che se accendi una luce chiaramente l'illuminazione si modifica – ma per aggiungere un'emozione all'immagine, per suggerire modulazioni emotive. Tarkovskij riteneva assolutamente interessante sfruttare il fattore temporale del piano sequenza, all'interno del quale si permetteva di modificare la luce, modulando emozioni e significati e aggiungendo così valore all'inquadratura. Voleva dei cambiamenti che non corrispondessero necessariamente a un processo esterno o ad una azione fisica». (Giuseppe Lanci)

NOSTALGHIA
Told by Director of Photography Giuseppe Lanci
edited by Monica Pollini, 2018

«Of the things that have stimulated me most, I would mention "dynamic photography", something I'd never seen before then. It involves modifying the lighting within a sequence plan, not for naturalistic reasons – like switching on a light, which clearly changes the lighting – but to add emotion to the image, to suggest emotional changes. Tarkovskij maintained that it was extremely interesting to exploit the time factor of the sequence plan, within which, by modulating the lighting, he modulated the emotions and significance of the sequence, thereby adding value. He wanted changes that did not necessarily follow any external process or physical action». (Giuseppe Lanci)

TONINO DELLI COLLI, MIO PADRE
Tra cinema e ricordi
di Stefano Delli Colli,
prefazione di Vittorio Storaro, 2017

Negli 80 anni dalla nascita di Cinecittà, che sono anche gli 80 anni dall'ingresso di Tonino Delli Colli negli stabilimenti di via Tuscolana 1055 –, Stefano Delli Colli, figlio del grande direttore della fotografia, rende omaggio al padre raccontandone, dal suo personale punto di vista, l'avventura cinematografica. Dal fervore degli anni '50 alla grande stagione al fianco di Pier Paolo Pasolini, da Sergio Leone a Federico Fellini, passando per Monicelli, Annaud, Polanski, Ferreri e tanti altri grandi registi, il racconto dell'autore, a tratti commosso, ci restituisce la memoria della parabola di uno dei "pionieri" della fotografia del cinema italiano. Un omaggio al suo grande mestiere, al suo naturale istinto fotografico, alla sua umiltà e umanità.

LA LUCE NECESSARIA
Conversazione con Luca Bigazzi
a cura di Alberto Spadafora
prefazione di Silvia Tarquini, 2012 - II ed. agg. 2014

Un libro intervista che "illumina" aspetti non noti delle migliori opere cinematografiche italiane degli ultimi trent'anni. La narrazione di Luca Bigazzi – direttore della fotografia e insieme operatore di macchina – raccoglie con coerenza caratteri tecnici, artistici ed etici del lavoro sul set. Bigazzi racconta la genesi del suo modo di lavorare libero da regole codificate, i motivi delle sue scelte professionali, la luce che ama, le ragioni della sua passione per lo stare in macchina. Come "controcampo", le testimonianze di 24 protagonisti del cinema italiano, tra registi, attori, produttori, fotografi di scena e collaboratori.

THE GREAT BEAUTY
Told by Director of Photography Luca Bigazzi
Alberto Spadafora (ed. by), 2014

Luca Bigazzi is one of Italy's most acclaimed award-winning directors of photography (DOP). His life has been dedicated entirely to the best of independent Italian cinema (not counting his work with Abbas Kiarostami). He has worked with directors such as Mario Martone, Gianni Amelio, Ciprì e Maresco, Silvio Soldini, Carlo Mazzacurati, Antonio Capuano, Leonardo Di Costanzo and Andrea Segre, and has been working with Paolo Sorrentino since *The Consequences of Love* in 2004. In this interview, edited by the photographer and film critic Alberto Spadafora, the Italian cinematographer talks about *The Great Beauty*, prizewinner of the Academy Award for Best Foreign Language Film of 2014.

PLACE, BODY, LIGHT
The Theatre of / Il teatro di Fabrizio Crisafulli.
1991-2022
edited by / a cura di Nika Tomasevic
foreword by / prefazione di Silvana Sinisi, 2023

Fabrizio Crisafulli's theatre research centres on Place, Body and Light, and challenges performance practices at their very foundations, in an attempt to reclaim the original potency of theatre and its relevance and effectiveness in contemporary times. This is where dance meets architecture, drama meets territory, and the performance of the body meets poetic light. Crisafulli's works – poetic and visionary, hypnotic and deeply emotional, full of life and irony – are revealed through interviews, personal accounts, critiques, information and photos related to performances and installations created between 1991 and 2022.

UN TEATRO APOCALITTICO
La ricerca teatrale di Giuliano Vasilicò negli anni Settanta
di Fabrizio Crisafulli,
prefazione di Dacia Maraini, 2017

Giuliano Vasilicò (1936-2015) è stato un protagonista del teatro italiano degli anni Settanta del Novecento, attivo nel particolare contesto delle "cantine romane". Nelle storie del teatro viene fatto spesso appartenere al cosiddetto "teatro-immagine". Un'etichetta – dal regista emiliano mai accettata – che, al di là della capacità che a suo tempo ha avuto di individuare un fenomeno e di farlo conoscere, ha poi forse fatto da deterrente alla conoscenza dei singoli artisti che di quel fenomeno sono stati parte. Il teatro è stato per Vasilicò un potenziale mezzo di rivelazione, innanzitutto a se stesso, di aspetti nascosti dell'esistenza. Da qui il titolo *Un teatro apocalittico*, visto che *apo-kalýptein* vuol dire togliere il velo, scoprire.

IL TEATRO DEI LUOGHI
Lo spettacolo generato dalla realtà di Fabrizio Crisafulli
con un testo su danza e luogo di Giovanna Summo,
prefazione Raimondo Guarino, 2015

Fabrizio Crisafulli analizza i caratteri della particolare ricerca che ha chiamato "teatro dei luoghi", a oltre vent'anni dalla sua prima formulazione. Un tipo di lavoro nel quale il "luogo" e l'insieme delle relazioni che lo costituiscono vengono assunti come matrice e "testo" della creazione teatrale. Le motivazioni alla base di questa ricerca, il suo riportare l'attenzione sui luoghi, la realtà locale, la prossimità, si sono riaffermate nel corso degli anni per l'accrescersi delle questioni legate alla perdita di contatto della vita quotidiana con i luoghi. Il "teatro dei luoghi", nell'uso comune a volte inteso (e frainteso) semplicemente come teatro che si svolge fuori dagli edifici teatrali, non è definito dallo spazio dove si fa lo spettacolo, ma dal modo specifico in cui il lavoro si relaziona al sito. Ponendolo come un modo radicalmente nuovo di fare e concepire il teatro.

ACTIVE LIGHT
Issues of Light in Contemporary Theatre
by Fabrizio Crisafulli
foreword by Dorita Hannah, 2013

This book looks at various important events relating to the poetics of light in theatre production in the West in the twentieth century, from the great reformists at the beginning of the century to contemporary artists such as Josef Svoboda, Alwin Nikolais and Robert Wilson. The intention isn't to outline a somewhat organised history of stage lighting, instead it is an attempt to identify some basic issues concerning its use. Lighting issues are unshackled from the limited contexts of technique and image, where they often end up only to be relegated, and examined in the context of the performance's space/time structure, poetic and dramatic construction, and the relationship with the performer. A section dedicated to the theatrical work of the author outlines the distinctive point of view behind the book.

LUMIERE ACTIVE
Poétiques de la lumière dans le théâtre contemporain
de Fabrizio Crisafulli
préface de Anne Surgers, 2015

Cet ouvrage revisite, du point de vue des poétiques de la lumière, quelques épisodes importants de la mise en scène théâtrale au XXe siècle, depuis les grands réformateurs des premières décennies jusqu'à divers artistes contemporains tels que Josef Svoboda, Alwin Nikolais, Robert Wilson. Non pour proposer une histoire plus ou moins organique de la lumière au théâtre, mais pour tenter de préciser, relativement à son utilisation, certaines questions fondamentales. S'affranchissant des contextes étroits de la technique et de l'image dans lesquels on tend souvent à les enfermer, les problématiques de la lumière sont examinées ici sous d'autres angles, ceux de la structure spatio-temporelle du spectacle, de la construction dramatique, de la création poétique, de l'action, du rapport avec le performer. Une partie de l'ouvrage est consacrée au travail théâtral de l'auteur. Elle documente le point de vue particulier sur lequel sa réflexion se fonde, point de vue suscité et enrichi par son expérience personnelle de metteur en scène.

Artdigiland has also published in Italian:

DA UNA PROSPETTIVA ECCEDENTE
In dialogo con Antonio Capuano
a cura di Armando Andria, Alessia Brandoni, Fabrizio Croce,
prefazione di Christian Raimo, 2022

Questo libro dialoga con la vulcanica personalità di Antonio Capuano e con la sua opera cinematografica, partendo dall'indissolubile commistione tra la sua dimensione artistica e quella personale, in un corpo a corpo con la sua storia, il suo mondo di appassionate preferenze e altrettanto radicali rifiuti, il suo sguardo singolare e sorgivo sulla vita e sul cinema. Composto da una lunga conversazione, nella prima parte, e da saggi critici nella seconda, il volume "fa esperienza" di Capuano approfondendo di volta in volta la regia e il rapporto con gli attori, la concezione del montaggio, la relazione con il paesaggio e con lo spazio urbano, il senso dell'inquadratura, la dialettica tra scrittura e realtà, l'assillo del tempo; incrociando così la vasta gamma di armonie e disarmonie di un percorso entusiasmante e vitale che eccede costantemente i margini. E rintracciando, come scrivono gli autori, «quel coraggio selvatico e quella autenticità materica che alimentano costantemente il bisogno di andare alla ricerca di una verità delle cose, dentro e fuori di sé»

IL SORPASSO. Viaggio nell'Italia del boom
a cura di Gerry Guida e Fabio Melleli
Prefazione di Oreste De Fornari
presentazione di Alessandro Gassmann (2022)

Il sorpasso è un film che ha saputo raccontare, meglio di qualsiasi trattato sociologico o testo storiografico, un momento epocale del nostro paese, quello del boom economico. A sessant'anni di distanza dalla sua prima uscita pubblica e in occasione del centenario della nascita del suo attore protagonista, Vittorio Gassman, questo volume torna a percorrerne le strade mettendo in evidenza i motivi per i quali è diventato un autentico cult-movie, scandagliando ogni aspetto della realizzazione e illustrandone il dietro le quinte attraverso testimonianze inedite di attori e tecnici.

INCHIOSTRO D'ARGENTO.
Immagini e parole
di Matteo Frasca e Stefano Talone, 2022

Quando le persone guardano le mie foto, voglio che si sentano come quando vogliono rileggere una riga di una poesia. (Robert Frank)
Leggere una riga di poesia riporta nella testa miriadi di attimi. L'attimo è il punto d'incontro tra il linguaggio della fotografia e quello della poesia. Su questo crinale è nata la collaborazione tra Stefano Talone e Matteo Frasca, il primo fotografo, il secondo poeta. Stefano, dopo aver letto Free Beats, una raccolta di poesie di Matteo, ha pensato a questa vicinanza tra fotografia e poesia. Per un anno i due hanno incrementato il materiale tra viaggi, esperienze, fotografie e parole, tra rime e pellicole. La particolarità della fotografia analogica, il fascino di scrivere ispirandosi all'immagine, la leggerezza di creare fotografie da poesie, sono raccolte in questo libro dove immagini e parole cercano un equilibrio.

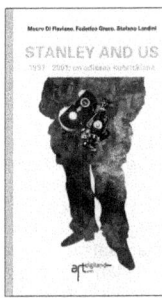

STANLEY AND US
1997 - 2001: un'odissea kubrickiana
introduzione di Federico Greco,
prefazione di Alexander Walker (2022)

Questo libro, aggiornato a quanto è accaduto fino a oggi, ripercorre nella prima parte le rocambolesche avventure dei "tre mangiaspaghetti italiani" – come furono apostrofati nel 1999 da alcuni scettici fan internazionali di Kubrick – che partirono alla volta dell'Inghilterra animati dal sogno di realizzare un documentario impossibile sul cineasta, Nella seconda parte propone dieci capitoli dedicati a vari aspetti della vita e dell'arte di Kubrick, attraverso le voci di circa cinquanta tra collaboratori, attori e famigliari.

È REALE?
Guida empatica del cinedocumentarista
a cura di Gianfranco Pannone
prefazione Caterina d'Amico, 2021
postfazione Daniele Vicari, 2021

È reale? Questa domanda potrebbe annunciare un saggio filosofico, ma nel libro c'è invece un'ambizione diversa: il desiderio, anche provocatorio, di rivolgersi non solo a chi si occupa di "cinema del reale", ma allo spettatore. Quello stesso spettatore che oggi spesso inciampa in una sempre più ambigua rappresentazione della realtà. Forte di un'esperienza trentennale e attento ai giovani aspiranti filmmakers, Pannone ci conduce in un originale percorso nell'appassionante lavoro del regista di documentari, che lui ama chiamare "cinedocumentarista", convinto che lo sguardo documentario sia legato non solo ai contenuti, come impone una vulgata lunga a morire, ma soprattutto al linguaggio delle immagini e al sapiente utilizzo creativo che se ne può fare.

CONVERSAZIONI SU FAVOLACCE
a cura di Ludovico Cantisani
con foto di set e disegni di Fabio e Damiano D'Innocenzo, 2021

Il libro ripercorre e indaga la creazione del film rivelazione del 2020 attraverso una serie di conversazioni e un esteso saggio del curatore. Le foto dei registi delineano un percorso ulteriore per scoprire la lavorazione di *Favolacce* ma soprattutto costituiscono un corpus d'autore che, attraverso un altro linguaggio, offre una chiave di lettura aggiuntiva dell'opera dei D'Innocenzo.
A discutere con Cantisani, oltre a i registi, sono: l'autore della fotografia Paolo Carnera, la montatrice Esmeralda Calabria, le scenografe Emita Frigato e Paola Peraro, il costumista Massimo Cantini Parrini, i produttori Agostino e Giuseppe Saccà, i direttori di casting Davide Zurolo e Gabriella Giannattasio, il colorist Andrea "Red" Baracca, e gli attori Barbara Chichiarelli, Ileana D'Ambra, Federico Majorana, Max Malatesta, Lino Musella, Max Tortora.

IL NERO DI GIOVANNI VENTO
Un film e un regista verso l'Italia plurale
di Leonardo De Franceschi, 2021

Da anni un'Italia plurale, figlia dell'incontro transculturale, inventa spazi di espressione, reclama diritti di cittadinanza, lavora per una decolonizzazione del presente e della Storia. È anzitutto a questa Italia che vuole parlare questo libro, che ricostruisce l'avventura di un cineasta, Giovanni Vento (1927-79), e del suo unico film di finzione, Il nero (1967). Con Il nero Vento lancia la sfida di raccontare, in una Napoli inedita, il coming of age di alcuni «giovani, italiani e stranieri, bianchi e neri», tra cui due «figli della guerra». Per il regista, queste migliaia di nate/i dall'incontro tra italiane e soldati della Quinta Armata erano «i primi neri della storia italiana». Nonostante una partitura audiovisuale modernista, le luci di Aiace Parolin e i riff di Piero Umiliani per Gato Barbieri, Il nero nel 1967 non riuscì a trovare un distributore. Dopo il restauro digitale del Museo Nazionale del Cinema, per questo film e per il suo autore, caduti ingiustamente nell'oblio, si aprono tempi nuovi.

PANE E CIOCCOLATA
Brusati, Manfredi e l'odissea della migrazione
a cura di Gerry Guida, Fabio Melelli
prefazione Andrea Occhipinti, 2021
in collaborazione con Archivio Franco Brusati e Lucky Red

Nel celebrare i cento anni dalla nascita di Nino Manfredi, questo libro racconta uno dei suoi film migliori, opera di un regista come Franco Brusati, tra i più sensibili del nostro cinema. L'odissea "ordinaria" della migrazione – nello specifico quella di un italiano in Svizzera – viene raccontata con toni ora comici ora drammatici, alternando momenti lirici a momenti decisamente più prosaici e arrivando a tratti al grottesco, ma con un impegno civile di fondo che rende la pellicola ancora oggi attualissima e dai risvolti universali. Attraverso una serie di saggi, una ricca raccolta di testimonianze dei protagonisti del set e i documenti messi a disposizione dall'archivio Brusati, il volume fa emergere le figure dei due eccezionali protagonisti.

CAFÈ EXPRESS
Viaggio in treno al termine della notte
a cura di Gerry Guida, Fabio Melelli
prefazione Alberto Crespi, 2021
Realizzato con il sostegno di Associazione Apassiferrati

In occasione del centenario della nascita di Nino Manfredi questo libro vuole invitare il lettore alla riscoperta di un capolavoro dimenticato del cinema italiano, un film che, agli albori degli anni '80, ha saputo raccontare l'Italia come pochi altri, ricorrendo alla metafora ferroviaria: treni e stazioni ci conducono nel cuore degli anni di piombo del Paese, tra povertà e cigolanti apparati statali, ben al di qua dell'immagine edonista e spensierata del decennio che si sarebbe affermata in seguito. Attento e acuto osservatore della società nazionale e dei suoi costumi, Nanni Loy sceglie Manfredi per rappresentare un venditore abusivo di caffè che nonostante le sfortunate contingenze lotta per sopravvivere, con sostanziale onestà, in un contesto sociale ostile. Ad arricchire l'analisi filmica i preziosi contributi del produttore, di alcuni dei protagonisti e della troupe, con particolare focus sul reparto fotografia.

L'APOCALISSE È UNA FESTA
Il cinema della fine del mondo e l'antropologia
di Ernesto de Martino
di Ludovico Cantisani, 2020

Passando dai blockbuster al cinema di autore più rigoroso, *L'Apocalisse è una festa* sviluppa un'analisi della fantascienza apocalittica e delle sue implicazioni archetipiche e culturali. Prendendo spunto da quanto tracciato da Ernesto de Martino nell'opera postuma *La fine del mondo*, ma tenendo conto anche della lezione di Girard e di quanto scritto da Jung a proposito degli Ufo, il saggio prende in esame un grande numero di film apocalittici, rileggendoli in un'ottica antropologica.

IL CIELO, L'ACQUA E IL GATTO
Il cinema secondo natura di Franco Piavoli
di Filippo Schillaci, 2020
in appendice le musiche originali di Luca Tessadrelli per *Nostos*

Un cinema sinfonico, una musica audiovisiva. Ovvero una forma filmica che ha saputo liberarsi dalla servitù della parola, del dialogo su cui si fonda il cinema narrativo convenzionale, per spaziare nei territori naturali dell'arte cinematografica, i territori dell'immagine e del suono. Un'arte non senza parole ma al di là delle parole: questo è il cinema di Franco Piavoli, autore per molti versi unico che, esplorando i vasti spazi della pura espressività audiovisiva, fonde la rappresentazione della vita umana con quella dei grandi orizzonti della Vita che circondano l'uomo, un universo alla cui rappresentazione il microcosmo squisitamente umano del linguaggio verbale è inadeguato. Un cinema fatto di elementi primigeni: cielo e terra, vita e morte, amore e conflitto, severità e gaiezza, felicità e dolore; tutto ciò in cui ogni essere vivente di questa Terra può riconoscersi. In altre parole un cinema il cui soggetto, un decennio dopo l'altro, è rimasto uno solo: quel «gioco bellissimo e allo stesso tempo terribile» che è il fenomeno della Vita.

MIRNA
di Corso Salani, dvd, 2017

Ultima opera di un cineasta anomalo come pochi e straordinariamente tenace, *Mirna* rappresenta la summa del cinema di Salani: storia di una donna, storia di un amore, storia di un viaggio e insieme sotterraneo autoritratto e sublime metafora dell'identità artistica. A partire da un incipit che ricorda quello de *La prima notte di quiete* di Valerio Zurlini, scivolando su acqua, paesaggio, musica e promettendo poesia, Salani realizza un cinema estremo, puro, libero, e scava con la sua camera in un'identità – la sua, dietro quella di Mirna – che misteriosamente si afferma con spontaneo coraggio e inevitabile autonomia. Il regista racconta nel volume *Mirna*, omonimo diario cinematografico che pubblichiamo parallelamente al dvd, che il film riguarda, come sempre nella sua opera, un tormento esistenziale reale e personale, un'esperienza di amore e abbandono, di ricordo, rimpianto, colpa. Corso Salani tesse trame sottili tra vita e opera, attua un transfert radicale nei suoi personaggi femminili, usa i luoghi come spazi dell'anima, come simboli, con un'attitudine che, prima di lui, era stata di Antonioni. (Silvia Tarquini)

MIRNA
Un diario cinematografico
di Corso Salani
postfazione di Grazia Paganelli, 2017

«Che poi, detto così, sembra soltanto un problema di casting, qualcosa che si risolve in fretta perché poi in fondo sono già stati fatti centinaia di migliaia di film in tutto il mondo e un modo per uscirne si trova, basta fare ricorso all'esperienza. Ma qui è un po' più complicato: c'è da presentarsi come regista straniero e chissà perché non c'è mai nessuna a cui venga in mente di dare un'occhiata su internet prima dell'incontro, anche solo per curiosità; c'è da proporre un film che non ha e non avrà sceneggiatura; e c'è da offrire un compenso che grida giustizia. E questo è il meno: anzi, non è niente. Perché la poveretta che verrà scelta, non sa – e non c'è modo di avvertirla prima – che verrà travolta in poche ore, al massimo dopo un giorno di riprese, da un'ammirazione, da una gratitudine, da un amore sconfinato che, come al solito, le toglierà il respiro e, tanto per citare qualche sua collega che l'ha preceduta – anime belle nel mondo delle meraviglie – perfino la libertà».

FUORINORMA
La via neosperimentale del cinema italiano
a cura di Adriano Aprà, 2019
Catalogo della seconda stagione del Festival Espanso Fuorinorma (Roma 2018-2019)

Il libro radiografa il cinema italiano indipendente e (neo)sperimentale degli ultimi 13 anni, di lungo, medio e cortometraggio, assai diverso e per molti versi agli antipodi di quello prodotto dall'industria. Film-prototipo, innovativi, che non hanno paura di andare controcorrente rispetto alle regole imposte dall'industria al cinema narrativo e a quello documentaristico in nome di un supposto gradimento del pubblico, che si rivolgono a spettatori pensanti e partecipanti anche emotivamente al "dialogo" proposto dagli autori.

IL MONDO VIVENTE
Conversazione con Eugene Green
a cura di Federico Francioni, 2017

Il giusto tempo di una conversazione per avvicinarsi a uno degli autori più particolari del panorama francese contemporaneo, Eugène Green. Artista proteiforme, approda al cinema dopo decenni di lavoro nella compagnia di teatro barocco da lui stesso fondata, le Théâtre de la Sapience. Il primo dei suoi sette film, *Toutes les nuits*, arriva nel 1999, quando Green ha oltre 50 anni. Da quel momento realizza sette lungometraggi e pubblica numerosi romanzi con Gallimard e altri editori. Americano di nascita e francese di adozione, riconosce la sua sostanziale venuta al mondo solo a 20 anni, quando raggiunge l'Europa e decide di trasferirsi a Parigi. È da qui che ha inizio la ricostruzione, la sua incessante quête di un linguaggio di cui sente l'assenza dalla nascita, lasciandosi alle spalle gli Stati Uniti, che chiama con il nome "La Barbarie". Il libro nasce dalla volontà di un incontro autentico, uno scambio, perché la storia del cinema è una storia di fantasmi e ombre. Di forme, ma soprattutto di uomini.

ADRIANA BERSELLI. L'AVVENTURA DEL COSTUME
Cinema, teatro, televisione, moda, design
a cura di Vittoria Caterina Caratozzolo, Silvia Tarquini, prefazione di Steve Della Casa, 2016

Un ritratto d'artista basato sull'immersione nella sua "fucina" creativa, e contestualmente la fisionomia di un mestiere. Dopo l'esordio, giovanissima, con Pabst, negli anni '50, Berselli è al fianco di Blasetti, Risi, Comencini, Vasile, Petroni e Camerini in numerosi film che ritraggono l'evoluzione della società italiana del boom economico. Michelangelo Antonioni le affida i costumi per *L'avventura*, trasparente capolavoro di analisi sociologica e antropologica. Negli anni '60 Berselli rappresenta la rivoluzione sessantottina e l'affermarsi di nuove tecniche, nuovi tessuti, nuove forme, prima tra tutte quella della minigonna. Nei '70 racconta le frustrazioni di un decennio già carico di fallimenti ideologici e politici. Ma il talento di Adriana Berselli non si limita al cinema...

RITA HAYWORTH
Cinema, danza, passione
di Claudio M. Valentinetti
prefazione di Lorenzo Pellizzari, 2014

Una sterminata filmografia, più di sessanta titoli, anche se pochi sono quelli folgoranti, *Sangue e arena*, *La signora di Shanghai*, *Gilda*. Cinque mariti, tra cui il genio Orson Welles e l'"imam" Ali Khan, e molti grandi partner sul set. Un mito costruito dalla Mecca del Cinema di quegli anni per mano di sapienti produttori e di abili registi: Charles Vidor, Rouben Mamoulian, Howard Hawks, William Dieterle, Henry Hathaway, Raul Walsh e, ovviamente, Welles. Una vita durissima: un lungo lavoro per raggiungere il successo, prima come ballerina e poi come attrice. Senza mai ottenere quello che più desiderava: la felicità familiare.

IL CALENDARIO DEL CINEMA
Ovvero L'altra faccia della Luna
365 giorni tra persone, film, momenti di riguardo
(e senza riguardo)
di Lorenzo Pellizzari, 2016

Un calendario che si rispetti dedica ognuno dei suoi 365 giorni a un cosiddetto santo o a un memorabile momento della liturgia. Poteva sfuggire alla regola un calendario dedicato all'empireo del cinema, all'Olimpo dei suoi divi e delle sue divine, agli eventi della sua ormai lunga storia? Non poteva. Persone, film, momenti, ripescati dalla memoria di un vecchio critico, con il dovuto riguardo per quanti se lo meritano e senza alcun riguardo per altri. Anche un modo per rievocare incontri personali, amici scomparsi, visioni effimere.

L'AVVENTURA DI UNO SPETTATORE
Italo Calvino e il cinema
a cura di Lorenzo Pellizzari, 2015
con saggi e autori vari

Nel trentennale della scomparsa, Artdigiland celebra Italo Calvino. Il libro ripercorre le poche ma fruttuose relazioni dello scrittore con il cinema italiano ma soprattutto sviluppa il viaggio in un immaginario che dal cinema prende le mosse. Si parte da quanto Calvino racconta nella sua *Autobiografia di uno spettatore*, del '74, prefazione al volume *Fellini: quattro film*, si attraversano racconti, romanzi, saggi critici individuando l'imprinting cinematografico, e si arriva al "segno calviniano" di non poche opere del cinema e del disegno animato contemporanei. L'apparato iconografico rende omaggio alla fascinazione calviniana per il cinema classico, soprattutto americano.

IL MIO ZAVATTINI
Incontri percorsi sopralluoghi
di Lorenzo Pellizzari, 2012

Il libro raccoglie quanto Pellizzari ha scritto e pensato su Zavattini da quando era ragazzo ad oggi, insieme ad una storica intervista, in cui Zavattini si concede forse come mai; documenta un lungo rapporto intellettuale e personale, fatto di infinite riflessioni, desideri, slanci, critiche, pentimenti, ripensamenti; e rivela l'ininterrotto impegno del critico a capire, da una parte, e a "stimolare", quasi, dall'altra, il suo personaggio. Un impegno appassionato e civile, e insieme sedotto dalla qualità giocosa della scrittura zavattiniana.

L'IMMAGINE COLORE
Le fer à cheval, un film Pathé
autori vari, a cura di / ed. by Marcello Seregni
prefazione di / foreword by Giulia Barini, 2016
in collaborazione con Ass. Cult. Hommelette e con il sostegno scientifico dell'AFRHC - Association française de recherche sur l'histoire du cinéma

Il libro propone una raccolta di saggi dedicati alla storia del cinema muto e al restauro del film, con particolare riferimento a *Le fer à cheval* (1909) di Camille de Morlhon, recentemente restaurato a cura di Associazione Culturale Hommelette e Fondation Jérôme Seydoux-Pathé. Hanno contribuito al volume Giulia Barini, Rossella Catanese, Eric Le Roy, Federico Pierotti, Alice Rispoli, Stéphanie Salmon, Claudio Santancini, Elisa Uffreduzzi, Giandomenico Zeppa.

UN LIBRO CHIAMATO CORPO
di Akira Kasai
a cura di Maria Pia D'Orazi, 2016

Le discipline esoteriche insegnano che il corpo non è mai un ostacolo per la piena realizzazione dell'individuo. Al contrario, è il mezzo necessario per la sua elevazione spirituale, perché lo spirito si forma per gradi dopo aver accolto ed elaborato le esperienze del mondo fisico. Ed è attraverso la focalizzazione della percezione sulle sensazioni fisiche che l'essere umano può acquisire consapevolezza della sua identità più profonda: allora, quando mette a tacere l'intelletto e dirige la coscienza sulle sensazioni, riesce a percepire il corpo interiore come un flusso di energia che scorre nell'organismo. Attraverso il contatto con l'Essenza è possibile distinguere i pensieri autenticamente individuali generati dal proprio sé, da quelli provenienti da istinti fisici o abitudini sociali; mentre si entra in un territorio senza limiti dove "io è un altro" e scompare ogni differenza fra individui, generazioni, civiltà o religioni che possa generare una cultura della sopraffazione e della violenza.

LE OMBRE CANTANO E PARLANO
Il passaggio dal muto al sonoro nel cinema italiano attraverso i periodici d'epoca (1927-1932)
di Stefania Carpiceci
prefazione di Adriano Aprà, vol. I, 2012

L'intento di questo libro è quello di indagare, in Italia, il passaggio dal cinema silenzioso delle origini ai nuovi fonofilm. A fare da mappa sono soprattutto le riviste e i periodici cinematografici nazionali d'epoca, analizzati a partire dal 1927 – anno della prima proiezione americana de *Il cantante di jazz*, pellicola che notoriamente decreta la nascita ufficiale e internazionale del cinema sonoro – fino al 1932, data di adozione del doppiaggio in Italia. Undici film sono poi scelti e analizzati come casi rappresentativi delle questioni messe in campo dal sonoro.

Artdigiland has recently inaugurated a series of Italian fiction:

**PIÙ OLTRE ANDAR
racconti
di Riccardo Garbetta
postfazione di Georges Didi-Huberman, 2022**

...È come se nei racconti di Riccardo Garbetta tutto si giocasse sul confine spesso invisibile – ma terribilmente pericoloso, aperto come un abisso – tra uno stato di fatto opprimente e un moto di desiderio che lo contraddice. Si tratta quasi sempre di *oltrepassare*, ma attraverso un *movimento infimo*: come in Borges, dove il minuscolo genera l'infinito, come in Kafka, dove il minimo gesto dà origine alle più grandi metamorfosi. (*Dalla postfazione di Georges Didi-Huberman*)

**IL PIANO DI LUCE
di Riccardo Garbetta
romanzo, 2021**

«Il vero dramma della nostra storia è di procedere sempre con cautela, per sottrazioni, reticenze, astensioni, di esporci solo ai devastanti effetti del non fare, non dire, non chiedere, non osare. Alla fine, quando nulla sarà accaduto, la storia si esaurirà nelle sue sole premesse; resterà solo la desolazione per i silenzi osservati, per le pulsioni inascoltate, i desideri repressi, soffocati, insultati. È con questo vuoto che le mie dita arrivano alle frenetiche misure finali, accanto alle quali hai annotato a matita *rallentare*».

Artdigiland is the publisher, in French, of the writer and filmmaker Marc Scialom:

MARC SCIALOM. IMPASSE DU CINEMA
Esilio, memoria, utopia / Exil, mémoire, utopie
a cura di / sous la direction de Mila Lazić, Silvia Tarquini
prefazione di / préface de Marco Bertozzi, 2012

Marc Scialom, ebreo di origini italiane, toscane, poi naturalizzato francese, nasce a Tunisi nel 1934. Dopo le persecuzioni naziste nel '43 in Tunisia, le ripercussioni sugli Italiani, meccanicamente associati al fascismo nel periodo dell'"epurazione", e la strage di Biserta (1961) – che denuncia nel corto *La parole perdue* (1969) –, si trasferisce in Francia. La sua vita si intreccia, "mancandola", con la storia del cinema: a Parigi il lungometraggio *Lettre à la prison* (1969-70), realizzato senza un produttore e quasi clandestinamente, non è sostenuto dai suoi amici cineasti, tra cui Chris Marker. Deluso, Scialom chiude il film in un cassetto. Torna alle sue origini, allo studio della lingua e della letteratura italiane. Traduce la *Divina Commedia* (Le Livre de Poche, 1996). Dopo il ritrovamento di *Lettre à la prison*, il restauro e la presentazione nel 2008 al Festival International du Documentaire di Marsiglia, Scialom torna al lavoro cinematografico con *Nuit sur la mer* (2012).

LES AUTRES ETOILES
de Marc Scialom
roman, préface de Frédérick Tristan, 2015

«Voici donc ce que je souhaitais réussir : le lecteur serait plus ou moins perdu tout au long de mon livre, perdu mais accroché, avec le sentiment croissant de frôler une chose intense, de l'entrevoir dans un brouillard, de supposer cette chose peut-être à tort, un peu comme un rêveur sur le point de s'éveiller voit parfois poindre à travers les volutes et sous les masques de son rêve une vérité douteuse, douteuse mais imminente, cela jusqu'aux dernières pages – puis tout à coup il comprendrait: rétrospectivement sa lecture indécise lui deviendrait claire parce qu'il découvrirait, lovée au coeur de la spirale et hors littérature, la scène première dont le livre est sorti».

Marc Scialom
INVENTION DU REEL
Trois contes
illustrations de Mélik Ouzani, 2016

Le réel est-il vrai ? Le vrai est-il réel ? Humoristiques mais graves, noirs mais flamboyants et bariolés, burlesques mais parfois terrifiants, ces contes ne peignent pas seulement un univers distinct du nôtre mais qui lui ressemble. À l'aveuglette et à tâtons, ils en esquissent aussi quelques possibles prolongements futurs...

LETTRE A LA PRISON DE MARC SCIALOM
Le film manquant
sous la direction de Mila Lazić, Silvia Tarquini
préface de Marco Bertozzi, 2014

Le livre présente, en français seulement, la partie consacrée à *Lettre à la prison* dans l'ouvrage bilingue – italien et français – *Marc Scialom. Impasse du cinéma. Esilio, memoria, utopie/ Exil, mémoire, utopie*, sous la direction de Mila Lazić et Silvia Tarquini (2012). Le livre source est consacré à l'œuvre de Scialom – cinématographique et littéraire – dans son ensemble, et approfondit sa relation avec la *Divine Comédie* de Dante Alighieri. Ce volume restitue à l'histoire du cinéma la mémoire historique et cinématographique cristallisée dans l'aventure, au sens antonionien, de Marc Scialom. Avec *Lettre à la prison* (1969) nous sommes confrontés à un film Nouvelle Vagues «trouvé», tourné avec une camera prêtée par Chris Marker, puis englouti dans un abîme bienprécis, personnel et historique. La préface de Marco Bertozzi cite Alberto Grifi, Chris Marker et Jean Rouch, filmmakers «dépaysés», constamment à la recherche, à travers le cinéma, d'un contact avec la réalité.

POURQUOI ?
Conte avec mort inopinée de son auteur
de Marc Scialom
libres dessins de Marcel Delmas, 2018

Vivien (mais s'appelle-t-il vraiment Vivien ?), un être mi-humain imaginé par un conteur fou que torture un lointain remords, s'interroge sur son identité profonde et, simultanément, soupçonne que l'espèce humaine est encore loin d'avoir achevé son hominisation. Plein d'une curiosité inquiète et sans cesse zigzagante, il part à la découverte des autres, du monde, du sens des choses et surtout de lui-même. Mais il découvre un monde second...

Artdigiland has published bilingually, in Italian and English:

MATERRE VR EXPERIENCE
Cinema Futuro Remoto | Past Future Cinema
a cura di/curated by Bruno Di Marino
prefazioni di/prefaces by Paolo Verri e
Paride Leporace, 2019

Artdigiland pubblica per Rete Cinema Basilicata e Matera Capitale Europea della Cultura 2019 il volume-catalogo, curato da Bruno Di Marino insieme alla mostra omonima, che documenta il lavoro svolto – sotto la direzione artistica di Antonello Faretta, Paolo Heritier e Lello Voce – per la realizzazione di *MaTerre*, film in realtà virtuale in cinque episodi girati a Matera. Il film nasce dall'incontro tra cinque videomaker e cinque poeti provenienti da culture linguistiche differenti ma unificate dalla civiltà mediterranea, e ha l'intento di intrecciare le matrici culturali lucane con la tradizione dello *spoken word*, da una parte, e con le più avanzate frontiere della ricerca visiva, dall'altra, mescolando innovazione e tradizione, oralità e tecnologia, memoria e immaginazione.

Artdigiland has published in English:

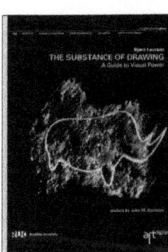

THE SUBSTANCE OF DRAWING
A Guide to Visual Power
by Bjorn Laursen
preface by John Kennedy, 2017

This book is not a manual as it is normally meant. It is not just a technical guide to learning how to draw. It lets you understand the motivations and impulses that are at the origin of drawing and the processes that are activated when you draw. And drawing is intended not so much as a simple tool, more or less effective, to imitate reality, but as a means of knowledge and memory with respect to reality. What Bjørn Laursen lets us understand is how listening and the availability to be captured by what we have around are essential qualities for an artist, and how the act of drawing is not a passive recording of objects, but a discovering and imagining, discovering the present and its history, and imaging the future of the environment we live in. (Fabrizio Crisafulli)

Artdigiland has published in Portuguese:

**RITA HAYWORTH
Cinema, dança, paixão
de Claudio M. Valentinetti
prefácio de João Lanari Bo, 2018**

A deusa do amor, a atômica, Gilda. O sonho proibido de muitos, a resposta vital à segunda guerra mundial. Rita Hayworth, talvez a beleza do star system hollywoodiano que mais fez época e clamor. Uma filmografia quase sem limites, mais de sessenta títulos, mesmo sendo poucos os que sobressaem, *Sangue e areia*, *A Dama de Shanghai*, *Gilda*. Cinco maridos, entre os quais o gênio Orson Welles e o "imam" Ali Khan, e muitos grandes parceiros nos sets, de James Cagney a Fred Astaire e Gene Kelly, de Tyrone Power a Frank Sinatra, de Robert Mitchum ao companheiro de muitos filmes e amigo Glenn Ford. Um mito construído pela Meca do Cinema daqueles anos e alguns expertos produtores – como o amigo/inimigo Harry Cohn da Columbia Pictures – e habilidosos diretores: Charles Vidor, Rouben Mamoulian, Howard Hawks, William Dieterle, Henry Hathaway, Raul Walsh e, obviamente, Welles. Mas uma vida desgraçada, desesperada. Após um duro e demorado trabalho para alcançar o sucesso, antes como dançarina, nos espetáculos e na escola de flamenco da sua família, os Dancing Cansinos, e depois como atriz. Uma diva que nunca obteve aquilo que sempre desejou e perseguiu mais do que qualquer outra coisa: a felicidade familiar.

www.ingramcontent.com/pod-product-compliance
Lightning Source LLC
Chambersburg PA
CBHW070733160426
43192CB00009B/1421